NCJ

The Struggle for Labor Loyalty

The Struggle for Labor Loyalty: Gompers, the A. F. of L., and the Pacifists, 1917-1920

Frank L. Grubbs, Jr.

Duke University Press   Durham, N. C.   1968

To Thomas Ashby Grubbs

Contents

Introduction

This book is a study of the struggle for labor loyalty waged by the supporters of President Wilson, represented by Samuel Gompers and the American Federation of Labor, against the anti-war Peoples Council of America for Democracy and Terms of Peace. From 1917 to 1920 the A.F. of L. sought to keep the American worker solidly behind the war effort and Wilson's peace policies in the face of the Peoples Council opposition.

Since the A.F. of L. was a far-flung organization of national unions, it was necessary for the Executive Committee to formulate its own loyalty agency, the American Alliance for Labor and Democracy, to unite labor behind the war effort. As president of the A.F. of L., Samuel Gompers organized and served as chairman of the Alliance, which under the directorship of Robert Maisel, a pro-war socialist, did important work in counteracting the pacifist propaganda of the Peoples Council chapters.

Although the declaration of war on April 6, 1917, at first threw American pacifists into confusion, by June the Peoples Council had been organized to agitate for a quick negotiated peace. The Council was directed by Louis P. Lochner, a pacifist of long standing, and Morris Hillquit, secretary of the Socialist party of America. The Council endorsed the peace proposals of socialist Russia and sought to disrupt the American war effort by urging workers to strike and otherwise interfere with the war industry. Before long the Council had become one of America's most militant anti-war organizations.

By July, 1917, Council pacifists had begun to infiltrate the locals of the Central Federated Union of New York City. Since many of these unions were members of the A.F. of L., Ernest Bohm, C.F.U. secretary, appealed to Samuel Gompers for aid in preventing a takeover by the pacifists. Gompers and those C.F.U. officials who supported the war hurriedly organized the American Alliance for Labor and Democracy.

The Alliance was created to pursue a dual role. First, its most obvious objective was to keep American workers impervious to the peace propaganda of the Peoples Council so that the Wilson Administration could enjoy labor's solid support of the war effort. Second, the Alliance was a subtle attempt by the A.F. of L. to gain continued labor reforms from the Wilson Administration and Congress. The A.F. of L. had supported the President since 1912. In return for this support, Wilson had been sympathetic to the Federation's demands for labor reforms under his New Freedom program. Now that the war had created a critical problem for the Administration at home and abroad, Gompers and the Federation were determined to demonstrate their loyalty to the government by giving their support to Congress and the President. This support, the A.F. of L. hoped, would bring the Federation a more powerful role in American society during the postwar years.

For their assistance in my preparation of this study, I owe a debt of gratitude to Mrs. Woodrow Wilson for allowing me to use the Wilson papers; to Norman Thomas for granting me an interview and allowing me to search the Norman Thomas papers; and to Scott Nearing, Jacob Panken, Louis P. Lochner, J. G. Phelps Stokes, Max Eastman, and Norman Thomas for corresponding. The library staffs of Swarthmore College, the State Historical Society of Wisconsin, Duke University Library, the Hoover War Memorial Library at Stanford, the Archives of the American Federation of Labor, the University of Virginia, the National Archives, and the Library of Congress were most helpful. Special gratitude is due the staff of the Tamiment Institute in New York City.

I appreciate the encouragement given to me in preparing this manuscript by Edward Younger, of the University of Virginia; Sarah Lemmon, of Meredith College; and William B. Hesseltine and O. Lawrence Burnette, Jr., then of the University of Wisconsin. Also gratitude is due Arthur S. Link of Princeton University for answering many of my questions concerning the labor policies of the Wilson Administration. And, lastly, I wish to express my appreciation to my wife and to my mother who aided me in typing and researching the vast amount of material incorporated in this work.

FRANK L. GRUBBS, JR.

Raleigh, North Carolina

The Struggle for Labor Loyalty

Chapter 1. The Background

The tragedy at Sarajevo on June 28, 1914, which plunged Europe into sudden war produced a crisis in the ranks of American labor. The nation's conservative unions, most of which belonged to the American Federation of Labor, tended to favor neutrality. The socialist unions also favored neutrality, but were deeply suspicious of the belligerents' war objectives. The remaining labor organizations differed widely in their opinions of the war, depending on their particular philosophies. Although confusion about the war was apparent throughout the labor movement, the A.F. of L., the country's largest federation, was more vulnerable to dissension than the other labor organizations. The A.F. of L. was a far-flung, loosely organized federation consisting of unions embracing almost every kind of labor philosophy. Under the direction of its dynamic president, Samuel Gompers, the Federation had progressed slowly but steadily toward organizing the country's skilled workers. In 1912 the A.F. of L. took the significant step of allying itself with the Wilson Administration and thereby working for its programs within the orthodox structure of the Democratic party.

The Federation's objective of welding together the country's numerous labor factions was seriously threatened by the war crisis. The unity of the A.F. of L. depended on the consensus of its unions; anything which tended to break down this consensus threatened the existence of the Federation. The European war touched off a crisis within the A.F. of L. as each union interpreted the war in its own way. As president of the Federation, Gompers was acutely aware of the dangers of dissension since he had faced a similar threat during the Spanish-American War in 1898 when some of the Federation's unions had opposed the war on the grounds that it was imperialistic. This attitude had concerned Gompers because it was basically the same as that taken by the socialist unions. A schism was prevented when the Federation refused to endorse America's assumption of the Spanish colonies. Now in 1914 the Federation faced a crisis far more serious than in 1898.

In 1914 the Socialist party of America took basically the same position as in 1898: it branded the war a "capitalistic" conflict among the nations of Western Europe. Since America was not directly involved, however, many socialists hesitated to come forth with a stronger accusation and chose to assume a watchful attitude.[1]

The decision to mildly condemn the war exposed a weakness in the socialists' ranks, for in 1914 the Socialist party was seriously divided between leftists and a large faction of moderates who openly endorsed nationalism. The history of this factionalism can be traced to the party's formation in 1901. By that year, the moderates, under the direction of Morris Hillquit, the dynamic leader of New York's socialists, had joined with the right-wing element led by the Austrian-born Victor Berger of Milwaukee; both men had successfully convinced the fiery leader of the left, Eugene Debs, to co-operate in the formation of a new coalition party. But hardly had Debs consented to join Hillquit and Berger when he deserted his moderate friends to aid in the formation of the extreme International Workers of the World. In true socialist fashion, however, Debs soon rejoined the moderates after the I.W.W. had proved too unmanageable even for his tastes.[2]

For a short time it appeared that this traditional socialist factionalism had taken a back seat to a more moderate approach which promised to pull America's middle-class progressives into the party. It was at this time that the socialists picked up the services of the millionaire New Yorker J. G. Phelps Stokes,[3] muckrakers William Bross Lloyd and Charles E. Russell,[4] and the British-born John Spargo, who believed in social gradualism.[5] Acting on the middle-ground philosophy of Hillquit and Berger, the party

1. There is a mass of material on American socialism. The most readable is David Shannon, *The Socialist Party of America: A History* (New York, 1955); the most analytical, D. D. Egbert and Stow Persons, eds., *Socialism and American Life* (2 vols.; Princeton, 1952), and Ira Kipnis, *The American Socialist Movement, 1892-1912* (New York, 1952). The party's position in 1914 on the war is discussed by Daniel Bell, "The Background and Development of Marxian Socialism in the United States," in Egbert and Persons, eds., *Socialism and American Life*, I, 314. (The Bell essay will be referred to hereinafter as "Background and Development.")

2. Kipnis, *The American Socialist Movement*, pp. 190-197.

3. New York *Daily Tribune*, July 13, 1906; Kipnis, *The American Socialist Movement*, p. 173.

4. Kipnis, *The American Socialist Movement*, p. 174; Morris Hillquit, *Loose Leaves from a Busy Life* (New York, 1934), pp. 56-60.

5. Kipnis, *The American Socialist Movement*, p. 202.

made important gains among America's foreign-born. Hillquit, now a recognized leader of the eastern faction, was instrumental in bringing into the party large numbers of German, Polish, and Russian Jews. At the same time, Berger's influence brought in large numbers of German, Slavic, and Italian groups from the Midwest.[6]

Despite continued criticism by the party's leftists, the socialists made significant gains from 1909 to 1912.[7] Membership increased to more than 200,000 and socialist candidates did well on the state and local levels, especially in the East and Midwest. The socialists also picked up considerable labor strength and by 1912 counted one hundred delegates within the conservative A.F. of L. Under the leadership of such men as J. Mahlon Barnes of the Cigar Makers International Union, the A.F. of L.'s socialists formed a small but noisy contingent.[8] With their membership increasing, the party was optimistic enough in 1912 to challenge the Democratic and Republican presidential candidates by nominating Debs to carry the socialists' banner. Debs hoped to poll more than one million votes and lead his party into national prominence.

But the election of 1912 proved to be unique in American presidential politics. Debs had to face a multitude of candidates, all of whom were reformers to one degree or another. The Democratic nominee, Governor Woodrow Wilson of New Jersey, was an active progressive who did not hesitate to call for a series of far-reaching reforms in his New Freedom program.[9] Likewise, former President Theodore Roosevelt sought re-election on his own brand of reform platform which he labeled the New Nationalism. And lastly, President William Howard Taft, a moderate Republican but a man who had built up the reputation of being

6. Arthur S. Link, *Wilson: The Struggle for Neutrality* (Princeton, 1960), III, 22-24; also Samuel Gompers, *Seventy Years of Life and Labor* (New York, 1919), II, 378-379. Gompers was fully aware of the importance of keeping the newly arrived immigrants loyal to American institutions.

7. Bell, "Background and Development," p. 308. For an analysis of the party's strength, see *ibid.*, pp. 291-292. See also Kipnis, *The American Socialist Movement*, pp. 335-336, and Norman Thomas, *A Socialist's Faith* (New York, 1951), p. 28.

8. New York *Call*, Nov. 11, 13, 1912.

9. Bell, "Background and Development," p. 302.

a vigorous trustbuster, decided to run again. To complicate the election, Samuel Gompers had visited Wilson in August and was so impressed with the candidate's promise to work for labor reforms that he personally endorsed the Democratic party ticket.[10] Faced with these three reform candidates and organized labor's opposition, the Socialist party was hard-pressed to sell its own reform program. Thus, when the final count had been tallied, Debs received an impressive 900,000 votes, but these were hardly enough to move the party into national prominence.

After Wilson's victory, the Socialist party's ranks began to thin. Many of its moderates flocked to the Democrats to work with Wilson's New Freedom and enjoy a measure of comfort and prestige previously unknown in the Socialist party. Party membership dropped sharply during the next few years from a high of 200,000 to a low of 77,000 after America's entry into the war. The inevitable resulted. Debs's failure to elevate the party to a position of authority in 1912, combined with the European war of 1914, released factionalism anew.[11] Many left-wingers deserted Debs and urged a revolutionary program, while Hillquit and Berger fought desperately to hold the party together.

While the Socialist party's strength declined, the A.F. of L. continued to gain strength among the country's skilled workers. By working with the Democratic party the Federation had shown its willingness to pursue a moderate course. This was especially true since the President had recognized the A.F. of L. as a powerful voting bloc. The Federation hoped that Wilson's need of labor's vote might eventually bring about closer co-operation with the government, a rapprochement which Gompers long had sought.

10. Gompers, *Seventy Years*, I, 544-545. Gompers had been suspicious of Wilson's lack of knowledge concerning labor's problems, but came away from his meeting satisfied that Wilson was deeply aware of the needs of the workingman. See also Arthur S. Link, *Wilson: The Road to the White House* (Princeton, 1954), I, 470-471.

11. Bell, "Background and Development," pp. 302-304. See also Kipnis, *The American Socialist Movement*, "The Peak of Socialist Power," pp. 335-369; New York *Call*, May 8, 1912; membership list, 1912-1914, Socialist Party of America, copy, National Office File No. 33, Socialist Party papers, Duke University Library, Durham, N. C. Norman Thomas passed off the factionalism within the party as comparable to a church congregational schism (*A Socialist's Faith*, p. 31).

Gompers had left England for the United States during the American Civil War. For a time he had flirted with socialism but had rejected that philosophy as a solution for labor's problems. By 1886 Gompers had aided in the formation of the American Federation of Labor at Columbus, Ohio. Since its beginnings the Federation had been composed of skilled unions committed to Gompers' moderate programs. From time to time, however, factionalism flared up within the Federation as the radical unions challenged Gompers' leadership. In 1893, 1894, and again in 1912 he and his supporters had to put down the Federation's dissidents.[12] Gompers' success in retaining control of the organization can be attributed to his personal magnetism, his skill in the use of parliamentary procedure, and his ability to rule by consensus. There is reason to believe that his presidency of the A.F. of L. seriously hampered the spread of socialism and extremism among American labor.[13] With Wilson's sympathy, Gompers hoped to accomplish a national program of sweeping labor reforms.[14]

At this point, war suddenly erupted in Europe. The American public was horrified at the destruction caused by the German army as it drove through Belgium and into northern France. The public noted especially the suffering of Europe's non-military populations.

The Socialist party reacted immediately and labeled the war a "capitalistic" one; but in reality America's socialists were shaken by the failure of their European brethren to prevent the war. The A.F. of L. was equally disturbed by the failure of European labor to declare its opposition to the conflict. Since 1898 Gompers, for one, had believed that modern warfare greatly hurt the labor movement.[15] The public's uncertainty over the causes of the war

12. Philip Taft, *The A.F. of L. in the Time of Gompers* (New York, 1957), pp. 125-126; Bell, "Background and Development," pp. 251-253.
13. Taft, *The A.F. of L. in the Time of Gompers*, pp. xvii-xviii. Taft suggests that the A.F. of L. prevented the spread of socialism by its conservative, non-political philosophy.
14. Wilson started his campaign in Buffalo on Labor Day, 1912. Gompers came out for Wilson in November. See Link, *Wilson: The Road to the White House*, I, 489-490, 500.
15. Bell, "Background and Development," p. 314. Some socialists were upset at the failure of their European brethren to prevent the war (*ibid.*, p. 308). Norman Thomas refers to the rise of nationalism as one reason why European socialists went along with the war (*A Socialist's Faith*, pp. 34-35).

increased as both the Central Powers and the Allies flooded the United States with propaganda justifying their roles in the conflict.[16] Consequently, neither the rank-and-file of the A.F. of L. nor the Socialist party was certain which belligerent was responsible for the catastrophe. Although the A.F. of L. was fearful of German autocracy, and the socialists were suspicious of the belligerents' war aims,[17] neither was willing to take a forceful stand on the issue until they had had more time to evaluate the situation.[18]

The lack of a decisive stand on the war by either Wilson, Gompers, or the socialists irritated America's latent pacifists who had been disorganized since 1898. Now with a new crisis brewing, all Americans who abhorred war enough to organize against it joined hands and demanded peace at any price. Pacifist socialists, progressives, and conservatives, regardless of their position in life, joined forces to demand that the President offer to mediate the war.[19] As time passed and Wilson failed to satisfy their demands, they formulated their own peace programs. Their constant agitation for a quick peace attracted many in the labor movement, and neither the A.F. of L. nor Wilson could ignore the fact that the pacifists' ranks were rapidly growing larger.[20]

During the fall of 1914 and the winter of 1915, a bewildering array of pacifist societies sprang up throughout the United States. Peace organizations appeared in New York, Chicago, San Francisco, and every major American city. The Woman's Peace party, the American Union Against Militarism, and the American Neutral Conference Committee of New York City were just a few of those which appeared overnight. Despite their variety, their pro-

16. Link believes that the propaganda efforts of the belligerents largely canceled out one another in the United States (*Wilson: The Struggle for Neutrality*, III, 35-40).

17. Gompers wrote later, "I was convinced that Germany was the real aggressor" (*Seventy Years*, II, 334). The Socialist party's position has been referred to in Bell, "Background and Development," p. 308.

18. Bell, "Background and Development," p. 309.

19. For an excellent introduction to the history of pacifism during World War I, see Donald Johnson, *The Challenge to American Freedom: World War I and the Rise of the Civil Liberties Union* (Lexington, Ky., 1963), pp. 1-21; also Jane Addams, *Peace and Bread in Time of War* (New York, 1945), p. 3.

20. Gompers' abandonment of pacifism is described in *Seventy Years*, II, 331-332; Link, *Wilson: The Struggle for Neutrality*, III, 53.

grams were basically the same—they all demanded a negotiated peace without victory.[21] As their numbers increased and their demands became more vocal, they clashed with those Americans who violently disagreed with pacifism and who were forming a vigorous preparedness movement.[22]

As the peace societies continued to develop, they attracted some of the country's most prominent individuals. Jane Addams, founder of Hull House, became one of the founders of the Woman's Peace party. Greatly influenced by the views of the Hungarian suffragette Madame Rosika Shwimmer, Miss Addams saw no reason why the women of America should not lead in the movement for peace.[23] Sympathetic with Miss Addams' point of view were an array of like-minded liberals. Paul Kellogg, editor of the *Survey*; Max Eastman, editor of the *Masses*; Norman Thomas, a young Presbyterian minister; Lillian Wald, founder of Henry Street House in New York City; Emily Balch, social worker; Henry Wadsworth Longfellow Dana, of Columbia University; and Louis P. Lochner, of Chicago—all flocked to one or another of these pacifist organizations.[24] Joining them was Rebecca Shelly, a slender young firebrand; Rabbi Stephen S. Wise of New York City, a prominent Jewish intellectual; and Stanford University's David Starr Jordan, one of America's foremost ichthyologists;

21. A good summary of the pacifist philosophy may be found in Randolph S. Bourne, *Towards an Enduring Peace: A Symposium of Peace Proposals and Programs, 1914-1916* (New York, 1917); also Devere Allen, *The Fight for Peace* (New York, 1930), and Merle Curti, *Peace or War: The American Struggle* (New York, 1936).

22. Link, *Wilson: The Struggle for Neutrality*, III, 137-138, and *Wilson: Confusion and Crisis* (Princeton, 1964), IV, 18; see also his chapter, "The Preparedness Controversy," IV, 15-54.

23. Addams, *Peace and Bread*, p. 7. Also the Addams papers at Swarthmore College, Swarthmore, Pa., contain much correspondence on Miss Addams' pacifist activities during 1914.

24. Link, *Wilson: The Struggle for Neutrality*, III, 165; *Wilson: Confusion and Crisis*, IV, 24-25. Paul Kellogg's *Survey* took an early stand against supplying munitions to the belligerents. Unfortunately much of this correspondence had been destroyed when the *Survey* papers were presented to the University of Minnesota Library at Minneapolis (Andrea Hinding to author, Oct. 15, 1965). See also membership list, "American Neutral Conference Committee of New York City," copy in Henry Wadsworth Longfellow Dana papers, Swarthmore Peace Collection. See also Robert E. Osgood, *Ideals and Self-Interest in American Foreign Policy* (Chicago, 1953), p. 241.

from California, too, came Republican Senator John D. Works, an influential West Coast progressive.[25]

At first these organizations waited to see if Wilson would mediate the war, but the President, regardless of his own feelings, hesitated to get involved in the bewildering European diplomacy of the day. Angered by Wilson's cautiousness, some of these pacifists resolved to seek peace on their own terms. In November, 1915, Jane Addams, Louis P. Lochner, and Rebecca Shelly led a group which encouraged industrialist Henry Ford to appeal to the neutral countries of Scandinavia to mediate the war.[26] In December of that year Ford decided to charter a Norwegian ship, the *Oskar II,* and sail for Scandinavia where Miss Addams believed the neutrals might sponsor a European peace conference. Ford's group met nothing but disappointment. The Scandinavians saw little chance of negotiating a peace with belligerents who believed that they could win the war.[27] The pacifists did not give up hope, however, despite the failure of their mission, and returned to the United States to seek other approaches to peace.

The opportunities for peace were slowly slipping from the pacifists' hands. In Berlin the German high command decided that a complete submarine blockade of the British Isles was essential for the winning of the war. The use of U-boats already had horrified the American public at the time the British passenger liner *Lusitania* was sunk in February, 1915, and the continued use of the submarine against neutral shipping, combined with an increasing number of German atrocity stories in the Allied press, turned

25. Jordan to Comstock, Oct. 20, 1918, David Starr Jordan papers, Hoover War Memorial Library, Stanford University. Jordan called Miss Shelly one of the "master-minds" of the peace movement. Also see Link, *Wilson: The Struggle for Neutrality,* III, 376. Senator John D. Works opposed making the sinking of the *Lusitania* a cause for war (Link, *Wilson: Confusion and Crisis,* IV, 336).

26. The correspondence between Jane Addams and H. W. L. Dana concerning the Ford peace mission may be found throughout the Dana and Addams papers at Swarthmore. Also see Addams, *Peace and Bread,* pp. 33-34.

27. Louis P. Lochner, *Henry Ford: America's Don Quixote* (New York, 1925), gives a detailed account of the mission from Lochner's point of view. See also Lochner, *Always the Unexpected* (New York, 1956), pp. 60-67. The Ford peace mission papers may be found in the Library of Congress, Washington, D. C. Colonel House thought Ford completely ignorant of the international situation (Link, *Wilson: Confusion and Crisis,* IV, 107).

the American public against the Central Powers. By the latter part of 1915, Gompers himself had become convinced that Germany must not win the war.[28] Public opinion was further excited against the Germans when the New York *World* published the contents of an official attaché pouch left carelessly on one of the city's elevated train cars by Doctor Heinrich F. Albert of the German embassy. The contents of this pouch hinted of numerous contacts between German agents and some Americans.[29]

Added to the rumors of German subversion in the United States were rumors of German subversion abroad. A proposed peace conference to be held in Zimmerwald, Switzerland, by a group of neutral socialists appeared to many Americans, including Gompers, to be another propaganda-inspired offensive to end the war on Germany's terms. The Zimmerwald idea was quickly endorsed by American socialists in their zeal for a negotiated peace. They urged the Wilson Administration to pay serious attention to the Zimmerwald meeting. However, the Zimmerwald conference failed to accomplish anything significant because the pacifist factions present could not agree on a definite program. By December, 1916, the pacifists tried again in Bern. Once more America's pacifists loudly endorsed the conference, and once more the American public saw the dark hand of Germany behind the movement.[30] This strong pacifist support of the international peace movement only served to convince Gompers that some Americans were outrightly disloyal to their country's best interests.[31]

By January, 1917, public opinion had swung decidedly in favor of the Allies. Because of this trend, a new peace society was hurriedly formed to prevent the Wilson Administration from entering the war on the side of the Allies. The Emergency Peace

28. Link, *Wilson: The Struggle for Neutrality*, III, 383. Wilson's fear of the submarine reached a peak after the sinking of the *Lusitania*. Link points out, too, that American public opinion started to swing against the Central Powers after the sinking (p. 43). See also Gompers, *Seventy Years*, II, 334-335.

29. Link, *Wilson: The Struggle for Neutrality*, III, 554-556.

30. On November 22, 1915, the Socialist party sent a message of endorsement for the Bern conference. See Olga Hess Gankin and H. H. Fisher, *The Bolsheviks and the World War* (Stanford, 1960), p. 364: see also pp. 309, 377, for an account of the Zimmerwald and Bern conferences and their tie with international socialism.

31. Gompers believed the international peace movement to be German-inspired to weaken Allied morale (*Seventy Years*, II, 391).

Federation held its first mass meeting in Chicago on February 27 and 28. Other rallies were planned for Washington, D.C., and San Francisco. The purpose of the E.P.F. was to ally quickly all American peace societies into a co-ordinated movement capable of blocking America's entrance into the war. Jane Addams, Rebecca Shelly, Louis P. Lochner, Editor A. W. Richer of *Pearson's Magazine*, Norman Thomas, David Starr Jordan, H. W. L. Dana, and Max Eastman were only some of those who actively supported the E.P.F.[32] Approximately two thousand pacifists attended the federation's Chicago convention and endorsed a program of emergency measures which included marching, speaking, and rallying until that time when Wilson would be convinced that the American people did not want war. Since there were indications that some of those present at Chicago were German sympathizers, the Emergency Peace Federation was branded a pro-German organization by the general public.[33] The inevitable resulted. The federation's Washington, D.C. headquarters was raided by a mob of soldiers and sailors, and Lochner's wife who was present at the time was warned not to interfere. When riding a streetcar, Lochner himself had had a copy of the *Volkszeitung* snatched from his hand.[34] Undaunted by the destruction of their Washington headquarters, the pacifists made a desperate last-minute attempt to see Wilson, but they were received coolly by the President and his personal secretary, Joseph P. Tumulty.[35] Nevertheless, they bombarded the

32. Emergency Peace Federation, membership list, copy in Dana papers. For the background of the Emergency Peace Federation's growth from the earlier pacifist movement, see Clayton R. Lusk, *Revolutionary Radicalism: Report of the Joint Legislative Committee of the State of New York* (Albany, 1920), I, 998-1022. This report will be cited hereinafter as Lusk *Report*. Also see Jordan to Comstock, Oct. 20, 1918, Jordan papers.

33. Lusk *Report*, I, 1014. Many congressmen refused to associate with the Emergency Peace Federation because of its pro-German taint (*ibid.*, I, 1015).

34. Lochner, *Always the Unexpected*, pp. 65-67. For background on German propaganda work in the United States prior to 1918, see J. P. Jones and P. M. Hollister, *The German Secret Service in America* (Boston, 1918).

35. Although Norman Thomas recalled that it was almost impossible for a pacifist to see Wilson (interview with author, July 7, 1964, New York City), Jane Addams and Professor Hull of Swarthmore College, along with a group of Emergency Peace Federation pacifists, did obtain an interview with the President just prior to the declaration of war in April, 1917. Wilson received the group coolly. Addams, *Peace and Bread*, pp. 63-65; New York *Call*, March 31, 1917.

White House with telegrams urging that America remain neutral.[36] Meanwhile, in New York City other E.P.F. members set about organizing the local Jewish elements under the leadership of two well-known rabbis, Judah L. Magnes, a brilliant young socialist-minded intellectual, and the progressively-minded Stephen S. Wise.[37] But time was running out for all men of peace; before the federation could either organize the East Side, influence President Wilson, or plan another series of rallies, Congress declared war on the Central Powers on April 6, 1917. The Emergency Peace Federation was now an organization without a purpose.

The Socialist party also was shaken severely by America's entry into the war. Although the party had been supporting the pacifist movement in the United States through the Chicago Peace Society, the New York American Neutral Conference Committee, and the Emergency Peace Federation,[38] socialists also had supported President Wilson's efforts at neutrality. Indeed, their support for the President had disgusted European leftists, who believed their American counterparts had sold out to capitalism.[39] But as the pressure for war grew stronger, the Socialist party

36. Jane Addams, Lillian Wald, Paul Kellogg, Max Eastman, and Norman Thomas were some of the few who sent telegrams to the White House urging Wilson to remain neutral. After the declaration of war these same pacifists sent the President telegrams urging him to protect America's traditional freedoms of assembly and speech. Telegrams may be found among the Norman Thomas papers, Box 2, New York Public Library (used with permission of Mr. Thomas). See also Addams and Dana papers; Jordan to Comstock, Oct. 20, 1918, Jordan papers; and E. C. Balch, memorandum, 1940, copy in Swarthmore Peace Collection. Wilson was fully aware of this pacifist agitation. See Ray Stannard Baker, *Woodrow Wilson: Life and Letters* (New York, 1937), VI, 500.
37. Moses Rischin, *The Promised City: New York Jews, 1870-1914* (Cambridge, Mass., 1962), pp. 242-243.
38. Jordan to Comstock, Oct. 20, 1918, Jordan papers. Norman Thomas recalled that the socialists wanted the support of the pacifist organizations (Thomas to author, June 18, 1964). For an account of socialist and pacifist co-operation, see Lusk *Report*, I, 515, 969; also William Z. Foster, *From Bryan to Stalin* (New York, 1937), p. 89.
39. Lenin wanted to use the Socialist party in the United States to start a revolutionary movement, but was blocked by the efforts of Hillquit and Debs. Frustrated, Lenin wrote, "and what is Eugene Debs? Occasionally he writes in a revolutionary manner" (cited in Gankin and Fisher, *The Bolsheviks and the World War*, p. 572). The Socialist party already had given its support to the Kerenski government of Russia (Socialist Party of America statement, April 2, 1917, copy, Swarthmore Peace Collection).

joined the E.P.F. in desperately trying to stem the rising hysteria which had become increasingly noticeable during the spring months. Socialists hopefully clung to a belief that Wilson would not declare war on the Central Powers because the President had once revealed that in his opinion the German people were not responsible for the actions of their military leaders.[40] But the socialists did not realize how disturbed the President was becoming over the sinking of American merchant vessels, or how persistent Secretary of State Lansing was becoming in his advocacy of American participation in the war.[41] The President's final agonizing decision for a declaration of war ended once and for all pacifist hopes of preventing the United States from siding with the Allies. Like the Emergency Peace Federation, the Socialist party had failed to convince the country that peace was more honorable than war.

Now that the United States had joined the Allies, the Socialist party was forced to re-evaluate its support of the Wilson Administration. Immediately the party called an emergency convention for St. Louis on April 7. The New York *Call*, the chief socialist organ in the country, termed the meeting the most important since the original formation of the party in 1901.[42] Once the leadership had gathered at St. Louis, Hillquit, Berger, and Debs demanded an outright condemnation of the Wilson Administration for betraying the American people by leading them into war. In the party's opinion Germany was no more to blame for the crisis in Europe than England or France; the war had been brought about by "capitalistic" competition. Since the majority of the party's leadership believed that Europe's labor organizations would be torn apart by the war, they declared they would not "give a single life or a single dollar" to the war effort.[43]

This anti-war declaration proved to be disastrous for the party.

40. David F. Houston, *Eight Years with Wilson's Cabinet* (New York, 1926), I, 305; also Baker, *Woodrow Wilson: Life and Letters*, VI, 118-121.
41. Link, *Wilson: Campaigns for Progressivism and Peace, 1916-1917*, V, 396-408.
42. New York *Call*, April 3, 1917.
43. *Ibid.*, April 10, 1917; Ray Ginger, *The Bending Cross* (New Brunswick, N. J., 1949) pp. 342-343; Executive Committee report, Socialist Party of America, St. Louis convention, April 7, 1917; Executive Committee minutes, Socialist Party of America, April 7, 1917, Document No. 15, National Office file, Socialist Party papers, Duke University.

All of its members were not as internationally minded as Hill-quit or Berger; some strongly believed in nationalism. These nationalists disagreed that America could ignore German autocracy. Of these, Winfield R. Gaylord of Wisconsin called the party's anti-war stand "un-American" and "un-socialist";[44] John Spargo agreed and begged his friends not to form an "obstructionist" movement; J. G. Phelps Stokes, Charles E. Russell, W. E. Walling, Chester Wright, and Robert Maisel of the New York *Call* also declared their objections to the party's strong resolution.[45] The anti-war faction under the direction of Hillquit considered this display of nationalism dangerous to the true nature of socialism. Hillquit was aware that nationalism had been the chief reason that Europe's socialists had failed to form a united front and block the arms race. He also had been disturbed by the failure of the German socialists to block Germany's large military budget in 1913. Likewise, neither the French nor the British socialists had objected to a similar arms buildup in their countries.

The failure of the European socialists to stave off the war only convinced the American socialists that they should not make the same mistakes. The Americans were convinced that their party must take a strong stand against nationalism at home and refuse to support the Wilson Administration. Thus, the anti-war socialists turned a deaf ear to the pleas of the pro-war minority not to obstruct the war. When a schism developed between the two factions, the pro-war minority submitted a report, written primarily by John Spargo, which objected to the majority's anti-war stand.[46] Shortly after the St. Louis convention, members of the pro-war faction began to leave the party. Only Hillquit, Berger, and Debs remained of the intelligentsia which had formed the party in 1901.[47]

44. J. L. Engdahl, "Minutes and Report to the Emergency National Convention of the Socialist Party of America," April 7, 1917, copy, Socialist Party file, Tamiment Institute.

45. Bell, "Background and Development," pp. 312-313.

46. Minority report, Socialist Party of America, St. Louis convention, in John Spargo papers, University of Vermont. The New York *Call* published the report on April 13, 1917. See also the *Call*'s issues for April 8-13 for an account of the pro- and anti-war factional struggle.

47. Bell, "Background and Development," p. 311. Memech Epstein is one of the few authors who feels that the desertion of the pro-war

Whether America's entry into the war would split conservative labor's ranks in the same way depended largely upon the A.F. of L.'s successful efforts at holding together its unions. Although America's direct involvement in the war had shaken the Federation, the majority of its unions favored the Allied cause—a sentiment which the A.F. of L. leadership accurately assessed. In 1914 Gompers, for one, realized that a firm stand for the war would alienate the unions and disrupt the Federation.[48] The A.F. of L. avoided the consequences of a showdown over the war issue by expressing a moderate attitude to its members, although Gompers personally believed that an Allied victory would be less harmful to European labor than a German victory. His attitude was fairly simple: autocracy and labor freedom could not co-exist. Throughout 1914, therefore, he supported the popular policy of neutralism because he feared that any other position at that time would be unpopular with the public. But he came out more openly in favor of preparedness in 1915 as the *Lusitania* incident allowed him to speak on the terrible consequences of a German military victory in Europe. Germany's increasing use of the submarine against neutral shipping, and the atrocity stories coming from Belgium, allowed the A.F. of L. to use public sentiment against Germany to educate its unions in the idea of preparedness. The Federation successfully backed Wilson's neutralist foreign policy during these critical months. The Socialist party's support of neutrality during 1914 and 1915 only aided the Federation in keeping down factionalism within its own organization.[49]

In Gompers' opinion the A.F. of L. could not be held solidly behind the Wilson Administration without some concrete promises for the betterment of labor. The Federation was too large and loosely organized, its membership too complex, to remain im-

socialists "little hurt" the party (*The Jews and Communism* [New York, 1959], p. 20).

48. Gompers, *Seventy Years*, "The Pitfalls of Pacifism," II, 334-349, and "Labor to the Fore," II, 350-359.

49. An excellent account of Gompers' realization that the A.F. of L. must co-operate with the war effort may be found in Marc Karson, *American Labor Unions and Politics, 1900-1918* (Carbondale, Ill., 1958), pp. 96-99. A study of Gompers' correspondence throughout 1914, 1915, and 1916 clearly shows his deliberate swing toward the Allied cause. See the Gompers papers, A.F. of L. Archives, Washington, D. C., and the Gompers copy books at the same location.

pervious to the cries of those who charged that the war had little to do with the world's working classes. Gompers believed that if the United States ever entered the war, the key to her successful effort would depend on the worker; and, if labor ever attempted to obstruct the war, the results would be disastrous for the A.F. of L. Gompers had spent too many years as president patiently aiding the Federation in its reform programs to see those efforts come to naught. The Federation in 1917 held the sympathy of President Wilson, and Gompers did not wish to lose this advantage. The leadership could make only one decision: labor must continue to support the government even if Wilson decided to send American troops to Europe; any other decision would damage the A.F. of L.'s image as a loyal federation.

And yet, labor's support of the war effort brought forth some serious problems. Gompers realized that history often had shown that during a time of crisis government autocracy had appeared in the most democratic of countries. Every government had found it necessary at one time or another to regulate wages, suppress strikes, and curtail labor's programs during times of national emergency. Labor had to be protected against the possibility that Wilson's administration would do likewise. Another problem concerned the attempts which were sure to be made by the pacifists and socialists to gain control of the Federation in order to obstruct the war effort. If the United States entered the war and things did not go well in Europe, Gompers might lose control of the presidency to those who always had asserted that America's intervention was a serious mistake. There were other problems as well. Business would naturally enjoy an elevated position during a war, and the situation would be ideal for management to pressure the government to suppress the labor movement. Indeed, the socialists had made much of this point and had openly accused Gompers as president of the A.F. of L. of placing labor at the mercy of business by supporting the Wilson Administration's policies.[50]

50. "Radical" opinion of Gompers' support of the war effort is wide and varied. See Oswald G. Villard, *Fighting Years: Memoirs of a Fighting Editor* (New York, 1939), pp. 353, 355. Lucy Lang was at first suspicious of Gompers' motives in working with Wilson but later became convinced that Gompers was right in co-operating with the Administration. See Lucy Lang, *Tomorrow Is Beautiful* (New York, 1948), p. 130. Other opinions may be found throughout the pages of Foster's *From Bryan to Stalin*, and Emma Goldman's *Living My Life* (New York, 1931).

Regardless of these dangers, Gompers believed that the Federation had more to gain by co-operating with the government than it had to lose. The Federation had backed President Wilson since 1912, and this support had already brought forth a favorable attitude toward labor in both the White House and Congress. Therefore, Gompers expected further labor reforms, and in May, 1916, he asserted that for its continued support of the government the A.F. of L. must have a voice in the national war policy as well as a voice in the future peace policy.[51] The President did not appear perturbed by the A.F. of L.'s demand. In fact, it was abundantly clear in August when Wilson appointed Gompers to the Advisory Commission of the important Council of National Defense[52] that Wilson was willing to placate the A.F. of L.—at least for the time being.[53] Later, in December, the Administration gave further evidence of its willingness to co-operate with labor by passing on to the German government the A.F. of L.'s official reactions to the European war.[54] Again on January 22, 1917, when the President made his suggestion for a peace without victory, he went out of his way to declare that he spoke for all forces of liberalism.[55]

When America entered the war, the A.F. of L. was shocked by the finality of the decision, but like the majority of Americans it accepted the President's decision.[56] The socialists, however, were disappointed that Gompers supported the action, and they

51. Gompers, "American Labor and a Constructive Settlement of the War," May 27, 1916, copy, Gompers papers.
52. Gompers, *Seventy Years*, II, 351-352. Gompers was advised by Secretary of Labor William B. Wilson to accept the advisory appointment.
53. G. B. Clarkson, a member of the Council of National Defense, believed that Gompers' appointment would gain the co-operation of organized labor. See Clarkson's *Industrial America in the World War: The Strategy Behind the Lines, 1917-1918* (New York, 1923), pp. 19-22, 280.
54. James F. Gerard to Gompers, Dec. 19, 1916, Gompers papers.
55. A. R. Leonard, *War Addresses of Woodrow Wilson* (New York, 1918), "Address to the United States Senate," pp. 3-12. Tumulty advised Wilson to give support to the A.F. of L. for fear that the socialists would gain the initiative in the labor movement. See John Blum, *Joe Tumulty and the Wilson Era* (Boston, 1951), pp. 142-147.
56. For some public reactions to Wilson's war message, see Clarkson, *Industrial America in the World War*, pp. 276-292; Lillian Symes and Travers Clement, *Rebel America: The Story of Social Revolt in the United States* (New York, 1934), p. 296; Arthur S. Link, *Woodrow Wilson and the Progressive Era* (New York, 1954), pp. 281-282.

raised the old charges that Gompers was a hyprocrite, a "class collaborator,"[57] and a leader who did not have the betterment of labor at heart.[58] Likewise, the pacifists were bitterly disappointed that the A.F. of L. had refused to aid them in obstructing the President's decision for war. But to Gompers this criticism meant little, for he did consider the government's support to be of supreme importance to the Federation's reform program.[59]

For his part, Wilson lost no time in laying plans to keep the public loyal to his administration. As the country mobilized for its first global conflict, the President ordered the creation of the Committee on Public Information with Denver newspaperman George Creel as its head. Creel had been a supporter of Wilson's since the election of 1912 and was an outstanding journalist. Secretary of State Lansing, a little shocked that the President could pick a liberal for the job, overlooked Wilson's desire to have the C.P.I. appeal especially to America's liberals. Creel made rapid progress in setting up the C.P.I. and was soon dispatching propaganda overseas to America's allies.[60]

By May, 1917, as a consequence of Wilson's decision to enter

57. Bell, "Background and Development," p. 255.
58. In a recent biography of Gompers, Bernard Mandel portrays him as an "economic opportunist." See *Samuel Gompers: A Biography* (Yellow Springs, Ohio, 1963), p. 358. "Immediate peace was just what Gompers did not want, he wanted immediate war" (pp. 357-360).
59. Gompers feared autocracy in the labor movement if the A.F. of L. did not support the President. Indeed, Wilson had declared in March, 1917, that it would require illiberalism at home to re-enforce the men at the front (Baker, *Woodrow Wilson: Life and Letters*, VI, 506. Yet with the co-operation of labor, Wilson hoped to keep the standards of conservative labor high during the wartime period (*ibid.*, VII, 52). Philip Taft believed that Gompers feared losing the initiative to the socialists if he did not loyally support the war (*The A.F. of L. in the Time of Gompers*, p. 344). For his part, Gompers feared that if the A.F. of L. did not support the government it would be ignored much as British labor had been during the early months of the war (*ibid.*, p. 347).
60. Lansing to Wilson, April 13, 1917, Wilson papers, Library of Congress (with the permission of the Wilson family). See also Robert Lansing, *War Memoirs* (New York, 1935), pp. 322-323. For Creel's account of the formation of the Committee on Public Information, see his *Rebel at Large* (New York, 1947), pp. 156-161. Also see the New York *Call*, April 26, 1917. For the best history of the C.P.I., see James R. Mock and Cedric Larson, *Words That Won the War: The Story of the Committee on Public Information, 1917-1919* (Princeton, 1939), pp. 10-11; Creel had supported Wilson in the *Rocky Mountain* (Denver) *News* in 1912.

the war, the domestic situation had been drastically changed. The Socialist party for the first time had taken a strong stand against the war and had promised to obstruct the war effort in every way short of revolution. The decision to become an obstructionist party may have driven some pro-war socialists away, but it also gave the party an unprecedented opportunity to exploit the situation for its own use. If the war proved unpopular at home, or if it went badly for the United States abroad, the party stood to gain, for the socialists long had warned Wilson not to get involved in the European conflict. Rumors circulated that the socialists were hurriedly putting together a new national anti-war program.[61] Other rumors had it that the President meant to placate the party by appointing some of its members to the forthcoming Root mission to Russia;[62] the White House, however, issued a vigorous denial.[63]

The domestic scene was further confused as the pro-war radicals searched for some way to support the war. Socialists Spargo, Walling, Stokes, and Russell all talked of establishing a more respectable movement based on a philosophy of gradualism.[64] Likewise, many of America's most prominent progressives, such as labor lawyers Frank P. Walsh and Clarence Darrow, who were sympathetic to socialism, now lined up behind the Wilson Administration.[65]

The most important remaining question, however, concerned the loyalty of the nation's skilled workers, the majority of whom were tied to the A.F. of L. In the confused times of 1917 there was no guarantee that these people could be held behind the war effort.

61. Wilfried R. Gaylord to Hustings, April 17, 1917, Wilson papers.
62. Gaylord to Hustings, telegram, April 28, 1917, *ibid.*
63. Tumulty to Hustings, April 27, 30, 1917, *ibid.*
64. New York *Call*, May 25, 1917.
65. Walsh's support of the Administration was puzzling to some liberals. See W. J. Tierney to Walsh, Nov. 17, 1917, and similar correspondence in the Frank P. Walsh papers, Committee on Industrial Relations, 1917-1919, Box 133, New York Public Library. Rabbi Stephen S. Wise deserted his socialist friends at this time also. Villard recalls that when Wise resigned from the American Union Against Militarism, "Sweat rolled down his face" (*Fighting Years*, 323-324); Paul Kellogg relates that Wise's resignation was "a struggle for a man's soul" (Kellogg to Addams, Feb. 9, 1917, Addams papers).

Chapter 2. The Revival of Pacifism

Shortly after America's entry into World War I, the A.F. of L. set about mobilizing for the trying days ahead. Gompers gave slight attention during these weeks to labor radicalism. The pacifists were demoralized when America entered the war, and the socialists were busily trying to reorganize their party after the desertion of the pro-war members. Labor pacifism did not increase further until the news reached America of a dramatic new peace plan advocated by the Bolsheviks. The Bolsheviks proposed that all belligerents accept a negotiated peace, that there be no annexations of territories taken, no indemnities for the losses suffered, and respect for the national origins of nations. This imaginative program served as a rallying point for America's pacifists and presented them with a much-needed chance to regroup their forces.[1]

When the Bolshevik program became known in America, many pacifists were greatly impressed with the solutions offered by the Russians for a quick end to the war. The plan seemed fair to all; it did not propose to punish any nation for starting the war, and it suggested that peace might be preserved by having the peoples involved determine their own governments and national boundaries. Thus, according to the Bolshevik formula, the major powers, Germany, France, and Russia, would retain their national territories, and, except for Austria, the European situation would revert back to a *status quo ante bellum*. The war could then be concluded with the great powers retaining their identity and no one power blamed for touching off the holocaust; the people of all nations then would be free to rebuild their political orders, and, as the Bolsheviks hoped, eventually their communistic societies. But what excited the anti-war labor radicals most about these proposals was their emphasis on a negotiated peace without victory. If some of America's pacifists had not considered the consequences of a communistic solution to the war, it was only because the Bolsheviks had not yet demonstrated their viciousness against the Russian people and because Bolshevism was little understood at this time in the United States.

1. For a complete study of the Bolsheviks, their origin and programs, see Gankin and Fisher, *The Bolsheviks and the World War*.

With the Bolshevik peace demands exciting their imaginations, the Executive Committee of the Emergency Peace Federation called a meeting at the Hotel Astor in New York City to consider how they could best propagandize the Russian proposals in the United States. On May 2 more than forty members of the federation, representing the Socialist party and numerous peace societies, gathered in New York to discuss the situation. But the meeting did not go smoothly, for soon a disagreement developed between those who advocated sponsoring the Bolshevik plan and those who wanted to create another peculiarly American peace program. Among those who sponsored the Bolshevik proposals were Morris Hillquit, Roger Baldwin, and Norman Thomas. Baldwin, as a member of the American Union Against Militarism, long had urged a more daring peace effort than his pacifist friends had been willing to accept.[2] Opposed to his views was the more moderate element led by Lillian Wald of the A.U.A.M. who feared that the sponsorship of an alien peace plan would brand the movement as a tool of a foreign government.[3] At the same time, Miss Wald objected to Baldwin's insistence that the movement needed the co-operation of the socialists, with Hillquit to act as liaison between the party and the pacifists. Despite the vigorous objections of the moderates, the extremists carried the meeting and proposed the establishment of a new peace agency to endorse the Bolshevik proposals.[4] When Miss Wald realized that she could do nothing to dissuade her friends from dropping their extreme plans, she urged her fellow A.U.A.M. members to retain their own identity by walking out of the meeting.[5] The remaining pacifists, however, quickly completed plans to set up an Organizing Committee for their movement. They elected Hillquit as chairman, and Louis P. Lochner as secretary. The Organizing Committee

2. Executive Committee minutes, American Union Against Militarism, April 4, 1917, copy, Norman Thomas papers, Box 2. Also see Johnson, *The Challenge to American Freedom*, for a thorough coverage of these early pacifist movements. The American Civil Liberties Union papers (microfilm) in the New York Public Library contain much on the attitude of these pacifists toward the Wilson Administration.
3. Johnson, *The Challenge to American Freedom*, p. 22.
4. Lusk *Report*, I, 1020-1022; Baldwin to Emily Balch, May 3, 1917, A.U.A.M. papers, Swarthmore; A.U.A.M. minutes, May 7, 1917, A.U.A.M. papers, Swarthmore.
5. Lusk *Report*, I, 1022; A.U.A.M. minutes, *ibid.*

was to form a new peace society based on the same pattern as the workingmen's councils of socialist Russia. Like their Russian counterparts, the American councils were to be run by their members through referendums. Officers were to be elected by the rank-and-file, and no important decision was to be made without first consulting the membership. The councils were to appeal primarily to the working classes and to those who were unconnected with the capitalist class.[6]

As secretary of the Organizing Committee, Lochner set about rallying support for the new pacifist organization. He counted heavily upon obtaining aid from the country's numerous pacifist organizations and influential progressives like Frank P. Walsh. Walsh often had sympathized with socialism, but he was now serving the Wilson Administration on the Industrial Relations Council of the Council of National Defense. When Lochner appealed to Walsh to join with the pacifists, Walsh refused to have anything to do with the radical movement.[7] Lochner then approached some of the nation's leading anti-war radicals. He met often with Morris Hillquit of the Socialist party, with Norman Thomas, with those anti-war members of the American Union Against Militarism who had rejected Lillian Wald's leadership, and with Rebecca Shelly, Lillan Secor, Elizabeth Freeman, and Rabbi Judah L. Magnes of the Emergency Peace Federation.[8] There is little information as to when or where these pacifists met, but the group succeeded in working out a program which welcomed any anti-war radical who wanted to obstruct the war effort.[9]

6. There were large numbers of German-Americans and Jews who were ready to join any movement to stop the war. See Carl Wittke, *German Americans and the World War* (Columbus, Ohio, 1936), pp. 3-4, 22; Epstein, *Jews and Communism*, pp. 3-20; and Villard, *Fighting Years*, pp. 322-323.

7. Frank P. Walsh to Lochner, May 26, 1917, Walsh papers, Box 15. Lillian Secor of the Emergency Peace Federation had tried to lure Walsh back into the peace movement as early as May 3 (Secor to Walsh, May 3, 1917, *ibid.*).

8. Norman Thomas to Grace Scribner, July 3, 1917, Thomas papers, Box 2.

9. Max Eastman to author, Oct. 31, 1960; Hillquit, *Loose Leaves*, p. 170. Hillquit vaguely records that "several informal conferences were held here and there . . ." between socialists and pacifists in the formation of the council movement. See also Lusk *Report*, I, 1020-1022. When asked about the lack of information on these meetings, Norman Thomas remarked that the telephone was an invaluable instrument for communica-

With the organizational plans proceeding well, the committee selected New York City as the site for their first meeting. Although the pacifists had difficulty in leasing a headquarters, largely because several pro-war landlords would not rent their premises for such a purpose, they had no trouble in obtaining Madison Square Garden for their gathering.[10] The committee was vitally interested in gaining an initial success by obtaining the services of a speaker well-known for his loyalty, yet one who was ardently in favor of peace. David Starr Jordan of Stanford University, an old friend of Lochner, a member of the Emergency Peace Federation, the American Peace Society, and the World Peace Confederation, was the first choice. There was good reason to believe that Jordan would gladly co-operate with the Organizing Committee and keynote the Madison Square Garden rally, for he had aptly summed up his philosophy in "There is no law of God or man which requires a nation to avenge a bad act by a worse one."[11] Since 1914 Jordan had been one of America's most eloquent pacifist speakers on both coasts. Early in 1917 he had come East to tour for the Emergency Peace Federation,[12] and he had made an impressive figure at the federation's Washington, D.C. rally in Convention Hall on April 2. He and John Milholland, a Republican, had presided before an audience of three thousand pacifists, along with a young socialist named John Reed, whom Jordan later described as being "a lovable fellow who wore out his life in a struggle—perhaps over-vehement—for freedom and justice."[13]

tion without leaving a record (interview with Thomas, July 7, 1964). Hillquit credits himself and Rabbi Magnes with formulating the council movement (*Loose Leaves*, p. 171); however, the Lusk *Report*, I, 1025, credits Rebecca Shelly, Lochner, Secor, and numerous others with being the driving force behind these meetings. The group informed Jane Addams of their progress (Lusk *Report*, I, 1031; Lochner to Balch, May 9, 1917, Emily Balch papers, Swarthmore Peace Collection.

10. New York City was known for its toleration of liberal causes (Clement and Symes, *Rebel America*, p. 302). Lochner had obtained a promise from Norman Thomas for a strong delegation from Boston. Lochner warned Emily Balch, however, that "Hillquit does not want to make this thing a talk fest" (Lochner to Balch, May 11, 1917, Emily Balch papers).

11. E. M. Burns, *David Starr Jordan: Prophet of Freedom* (Stanford, 1953), p. 28.

12. *Ibid.*, p. 30.

13. David Starr Jordan, *The Days of a Man* (New York, 1922), II, 726-731.

Lochner wrote Jordan on May 5 and explained that he was organizing a new peace movement to stage "The First American Conference for Democracy and Terms of Peace" in Madison Square Garden later that month. This rally, Lochner pointed out, would present new plans to agitate for an end to the war by adopting the Bolshevik peace proposals. The entire effort, Lochner insisted, lay within the traditional American pacifist movement and would need a prominent speaker like Jordan to keynote the first rally.[14] Although Jordan had been unfamiliar with the council idea, he had known Lochner for some years as a faithful pacifist who had associated with many of his own friends. Yet Jordan was bothered by the presence of so many socialists in the movement and was interested especially in Morris Hillquit's role in the organization.[15]

While Jordan debated whether to join the council movement or not, Lochner appealed to the A.F. of L.'s Executive Committee to support the New York rally.[16] His telegram to Gompers caught the A.F. of L. chief at a time when he was engaged in the hectic task of converting the Federation to a wartime footing, and Gompers angrily shot back, "I prefer not to ally myself with the conscious or unconscious agents of the Kaiser in America."[17] Gompers' curt refusal to aid the pacifists drew widespread approval from the nation's loyal press, which congratulated him upon his "brief, stabbing message" and for being "a true American who stands clean in the present war crisis."[18] At a time when the government was becoming increasingly concerned over the resurgence of labor pacifism, Gompers' stand could not have created a better image for the A.F. of L.[19]

But Gompers' refusal to participate in the New York rally did not slow down the efforts of the Organizing Committee. By May

14. Lochner to Jordan, telegram, May 5, 1917, Jordan papers.
15. Jordan to Comstock, Oct. 20, 1918, *ibid*.
16. Lusk *Report*, I, 1032-1033.
17. Gompers to Lochner, telegram, May 10, 1917, Gompers papers.
18. New York *Times*, May 11, 12, 1917; Chicago *Tribune*, May 12, 1917; Washington *Herald*, May 12, 1917; Albany *Telegram*, May 12, 1917; Worcester *Times*, May 11, 1917, copies in Gompers papers.
19. Wilson wrote to Lansing on May 11, 1917: "I do not like the movement among the socialists to confer about international affairs. They are likely to make a great deal of mischief, especially in connection with affairs in Russia" (Baker, *Woodrow Wilson: Life and Letters*, VII, 65).

14 Lochner had set up a Program Committee consisting of himself, Hillquit, H. W. L. Dana of Columbia University, Norman Thomas, Rebecca Shelly, and Elizabeth Freeman.[20] The committee unhesitatingly decided to endorse the Bolshevik peace demands and to co-operate with the Socialist party's anti-war program which called for vigorous opposition to any suppression of labor, to federal censorship, and to conscription.[21] Once again Lochner appealed to Jordan to speak at the New York rally by asking him to come to New York and see for himself "that the council pacifists are interested only in stopping the needless bloodshed in Europe."[22] He suggested that Jordan, who already was preparing to come East on other business, visit Council headquarters in New York and familiarize himself with the organization.[23]

But before Jordan could come East, an incident occurred which focused the public's attention on the movement and greatly added to its notoriety in the press. The Socialist party and many pacifists previously had endorsed the defunct Zimmerwald movement of 1915, as well as the Bern conference of 1916. Now, a new international peace convention had been called for Stockholm in the late summer. The Socialist party was quick to endorse this conference, and numerous pacifist organizations followed their lead. Before the party could dispatch its elected delegates—Hillquit, Berger, Algernon Lee, and James H. Maurer, president of the Pennsylvania Federation of Labor—to Sweden, they first had to obtain State Department clearance because no one was allowed to travel to Europe at that time without Secretary Lansing's special permission. Lansing, moreover, was against allowing these

20. For a detailed list of those who took part in the original founding of the council movement, see Lusk *Report*, I, 1031-1032.
21. "Committee for the First American Conference for Democracy and Terms of Peace," report, May 14, 1917, copy in Swarthmore Peace Collection. President Wilson was well aware that the radicals might try to exploit the labor situation. On May 15, 1917, the President wrote: "We are trying to fight the cause which means the lifting of the standards of life, and we can fight in that cause best by voluntary cooperation . . ." (Baker, *Woodrow Wilson: Life and Letters*, VII, 69). Rabbi Magnes at first did not want the pacifists to discuss anything except labor problems and living conditions (Lochner to Balch, May 18, 1917, Emily Balch papers, Swarthmore). Rebecca Shelly called the meetings the most important "since the declaration of war" (Shelly to Dana, May 22, 1917, Dana papers).
22. Lochner to Jordan, May 14, 1917, Jordan papers.
23. Jordan, *Days of a Man*, II, 734-747.

delegates to fraternize with alien socialists. The President's feelings were similar and he needed no encouragement from Lansing to restrict the delegates' travel plans. Wilson feared that if the Stockholm conference endorsed the Bolshevik proposals, the action might swing the balance of power within Russia over to the extremists.[24] Consequently, Lansing refused to approve the issuance of passports to the delegates. A few days later Wilson attacked those calling for a negotiated peace by declaring that America's war aims "had been clouded during the last few weeks by mistaken and misleading statements." The President promised the American people that there would be no hasty negotiated peace in Europe.[25]

Angered by Wilson's refusal to allow its delegates to leave the country, the Socialist party unleashed a bitter attack upon the Administration for restricting freedom of action. The Council pacifists joined this attack by agreeing to air the entire issue at their New York rally. In preparation for this rally, Lochner asked a leading spokesman on internationalism, Professor William I. Hull of Swarthmore College, to speak on the necessity of bringing about peace through the co-operation of all nations, both belligerent and neutral.[26] This disagreement between the government and the Socialist party was publicized from coast to coast in the nation's press just as Jordan prepared to leave for the East.

In the meantime, Lochner managed to bring two of America's most outstanding pacifists into the council movement. Emily Green Balch, a political economist and respected peace advocate who was to win the Nobel Peace Prize in 1946, and Scott Nearing, former dean of Toledo University, joined the movement's ranks. Nearing lost no time in declaring that he favored making the council movement more than just a local rally. He envisioned extending the movement into a national organization capable of

24. Baker, *Woodrow Wilson: Life and Letters*, VII, 84 n. Lansing advised Wilson against allowing the socialists to depart from the United States on May 19, 1917. For a discussion of the Stockholm conferences from the labor point of view, see L. L. Lorwin, *The International Labor Movement* (New York, 1953), pp. 47-49, and *Labor and Internationalism* (New York, 1929), pp. 149-162.

25. Albert Shaw, ed., *Messages and Papers of Woodrow Wilson* (New York, 1924), I, 405-406.

26. Lochner to Hull, May 24, 1917, William I. Hull papers, Swarthmore Peace Collection.

organizing every anti-war group in the country. He also advised close co-operation with the Socialist party's obstructionist program. Nearing's suggestions gained immediate support from Rebecca Shelly, Hillquit, Lochner, and Roger Baldwin, all of whom enthusiastically endorsed this broadened concept of the council idea.[27] Under Nearing's direction, the Organizing Committee decided to expand its program to set up councils in Philadelphia, Los Angeles, San Francisco, Salt Lake City, Seattle, and Chicago.[28]

These changes necessitated approval from the entire membership, and Lochner, Rebecca Shelly, and Nearing set about drawing up a resolution to expand the council idea into a national movement. Plans were made to have Rebecca Shelly offer the resolution to the Madison Square Garden rally after the audience had been exposed to two days of anti-war speeches. The First American Conference for Democracy and Terms of Peace took on an added significance. Council leaders now were prepared to turn what had been previously a local protest rally into a national peace movement consisting of workingmen's councils from coast to coast. It was clear that the Socialist party, represented physically in the council movement by Morris Hillquit, would be prepared to give the pacifists all the support it could muster.[29]

Against this background, the First American Conference for Democracy and Terms of Peace opened on the morning of May 30 with a flurry of excitement and apprehension.[30] Although

27. *American Federation of Labor: History, Encyclopedia, References* (Washington, D. C., 1919), pp. 72-74; Lusk *Report*, I, 1037; Hillquit, *Loose Leaves*, p. 171. Hillquit called Miss Shelly "the Maid of Orleans. . . ."

28. Rabbi Magnes directed the movement during this period while Lochner was ill. See American Union Against Militarism minutes, May 28, 1917, A.U.A.M. papers. Although the A.U.A.M. refused to become a part of the Council, it did give its co-operation in the New York rally (New York *Call*, May 29, 1917).

29. See Alexander Trachtenberg, ed., *The American Labor Year Book, 1919-1920* (New York, 1920), pp. 80-83, for a history of the council movement as written by H. W. L. Dana. Hillquit is believed to have given the word that the Socialist party would co-operate in every way with the Council (Lusk *Report*, I, 1020).

30. The New York *Call*, May 29, 1917, contains a large advertisement for the May 30-31 rally which is signed by Hillquit, Algernon Lee, Victor Berger, David Starr Jordan, Scott Nearing, W. I. Hull, H. W. L. Dana, Job Harriman, Harry Laidler, and Benjamin Schlossberg.

heralded as a peaceful gathering of pacifists, the rally was heavily guarded by the New York City police who feared everything from mob violence to revolution. Elaborate precautions were taken to preserve order. Patrolmen armed with riot guns were massed on the street corners surrounding the Garden. At night floodlights illuminated the area outside and police trucks equipped with searchlights drove through the streets. More than four hundred police stood guard against the possibility of trouble.[31]

These precautions, however, did not dampen the spirits of the crowds, and approximately twenty thousand pacifists filed into the Garden during the next two days. The first session began at 10 A.M. with Dr. Judah L. Magnes presiding over four hundred delegates who began work on a preamble calling on all Americans to "Aid our government in bringing to ourselves and the world a speedy, righteous, and lasting peace." The group officially endorsed the Bolshevik peace demands of no annexation, no indemnities, and the self-determination of all peoples, expressed disapproval of the government's attempts to suppress freedom of speech and assembly, condemned the Conscription Act of May 18, and proclaimed themselves the champions of organized labor.[32]

Magnes spurred the delegates on with a stirring speech in which he appealed to Wilson to seek a speedy negotiated settlement of the war as well as to declare America's war aims. The liberal rabbi hinted that perhaps the Administration was fighting only to preserve capitalism in Western Europe. Heartily endorsing the Bolshevik proposal, Magnes bitterly attacked Britain and France for pursuing a war which offered little to the working peoples of the world. The council movement, he declared, was on the side of the common man as it sought a peace acceptable to all.[33] Magnes' speech was well-received by the delegates who loudly applauded his views.[34] Later when the Council distributed fifty thousand copies of this address throughout the country, the

31. Hillquit, *Loose Leaves*, pp. 170-171; New York *Times*, May 31, June 1, 1917.

32. New York *Times*, May 31, 1917; First American Conference for Democracy and Terms of Peace, report, May 30, 1917, first session, copy, Peoples Council of America file, Tamiment Institute.

33. J. L. Magnes, speech, May 30, 1917, copy, Swarthmore Peace Collection.

34. New York *Call*, May 31, 1917.

Justice Department declared it seditious, banned it from the mails, and added Magnes' name to its growing list of radicals.[35]

Magnes turned the lectern over to Algernon Lee of the Socialist party, who informed the delegates of the latest efforts to bring about a peace convention at Stockholm. Lee then read a statement from Morris Hillquit, who had been unable to attend the session, which endorsed the Stockholm idea and proposed a new plan to ensure a negotiated peace. Hillquit proposed that at a world peace conference the Allied nations be given 123 votes, the Central Powers fifty, and the neutral countries forty-eight votes. He suggested that such a system would ensure the major belligerents the most votes and the lesser ones the least. This allocation of votes, he declared, would ensure a fair distribution and would even give the Allies a slight advantage. He also urged the establishment of an international trade board which would adjust all future economic grievances before they could erupt into war.[36] Hillquit's proposals, as read by Lee, were widely acclaimed by the delegates as a constructive move toward bringing the Stockholm idea into reality.

The afternoon session got under way at 3 P.M. with an address by Professor William I. Hull, who ironically enough had been a student of President Wilson's.[37] Pointing out that George Washington had warned Americans not to become involved in foreign disputes, Hull cautioned Wilson against making any secret agreements with the Allies which might commit the United States to another war. He also called for an international conference of nations to decide the peace. Hull was followed by Victor Berger, who bitterly condemned the business community for profiteering from the war, creating monopolies, and holding down wages. Berger said that the American people would never tolerate profiteering, especially as America's sons were dying on the battlefields of Europe. He warned Wilson that if he did not give more

35. Rabbi Magnes' speech was considered seditious by Postmaster General Burleson, who turned a copy of it over to the Justice Department (J. C. Koons to Secretary of State Lansing, June 4, 1917, copy in Postmaster General's papers, National Archives, Washington, D. C.).

36. First American Conference for Democracy and Terms of Peace, report, May 30, 1917, first session, copy, P.C.A. file, Tamiment Institute.

37. *Ibid.* Dr. Hull had earlier written *Preparedness: The American vs. Military Programme* (New York, 1916).

attention to the domestic needs of the country, there would be riots from coast to coast. As for Stockholm, Berger declared that he planned to attend the conference despite the opposition of the Administration.[38]

That night, while searchlights scanned the area outside the Garden, James Maurer opened the session on labor. Beginning with a severe denunciation of his old enemy Samuel Gompers, Maurer charged that Gompers had sold out the labor movement to capitalism. Maurer offered the council idea as the only way that America's workers could achieve an industrial democracy.[39] He urged the delegates to support the Socialist party and the Council until a truly liberal labor movement could be built. Maurer was followed by Scott Nearing, who told the delegates that if the country did not support a liberal labor movement, America's workers would be intolerably suppressed by the government during the long years of war. After Nearing's speech, the first day's session ended with Treasurer Elizabeth Freeman collecting voluntary donations for the Council's programs.[40]

Early the next morning (May 31) the pacifists hurried back into the Garden for the opening of the final day of the rally. Florence Kelley, a well-known industrial sociologist, appealed for the Wilson Administration to improve labor's working conditions and to protect labor against unfair employment practices during wartime. The remaining hours were filled with numerous speakers who called for a repeal of the Conscription Act and an endorsement of the Bolshevik proposals.

But the most critical session came that afternoon when Re-

38. Berger had appealed to Secretary Lansing on May 28, 1917, for a passport to Stockholm. Lansing noted that "Victor Berger made out a poor case" (Lansing, desk diaries, II, 148, Lansing papers, Library of Congress). First American Conference for Democracy and Terms of Peace, report, May 30, 1917, second session, copy, P.C.A. file, Tamiment Institute.

39. Scott Nearing considered Maurer one of the most influential members of the council movement (Nearing to author, Oct. 26, 1960).

40. First American Conference for Democracy and Terms of Peace, report, May 30, 1917, third session, Tamiment Institute. The New York *Call*, May 31, 1917, has good coverage of the meetings. The *Call* correspondent wrote that the pacifists would help "preserve the democracy upon which America had prided herself," and "would oppose the artificial war hysteria which threatened to tear down the democracy which it had taken generations to build up." The writer predicted that "a national-wide assault on labor's standards will now begin."

becca Shelly presented the "Suggestions for the Peoples Council of America." This proposal called for the establishment of a national council movement composed of locals modeled after those in Russia and operated through a system of universal suffrage and national referendums. Miss Shelly urged that a national convention, composed of delegates from these locals, be held in the fall. Each delegate would represent one thousand members who would be dedicated to the Bolshevik peace principles and a liberal labor movement. She suggested that the convention be held in the Midwest on September 1, that a national office be set up afterward in Washington, D.C., and that a Council bulletin be distributed throughout the country. In asking the delegates to endorse the "Suggestions," Miss Shelly pointed out that the government was beginning to censor freedom of speech, and "a non-partisan organization was now needed to act as an agency through which our European friends can speak to America." If there had been any doubt as to whether the council idea would appeal to the delegates, it was soon dispelled, for they enthusiastically called for the creation of a national movement.[41]

The First American Conference for Democracy and Terms of Peace ended that night with a giant peace rally. While police stood ready for trouble, a large crowd of pacifists gathered inside. James Maurer again spoke on the importance of safeguarding labor's wartime rights, and Max Eastman, who earlier had been much impressed by Magnes' opening speech, repeated many of the same charges against Wilson for leading the country into war. The two-day session ended on a note of renewed hope that the council movement could arouse enough opposition to America's participation in the war to force a quick negotiated peace. For the pacifists the two-day rally had been conducted with a minimum of disturbance. The only disorder had been a minor one when a group of servicemen had paraded down to the lectern waving an American flag to protest a statement by Maurer that

41. "Suggestions for the Formation of the Peoples Council of America," copy, P.C.A. file, New York Public Library; also First American Conference for Democracy and Terms of Peace, report, May 31, 1917, Tamiment Institute. Hillquit gives a dramatic account of Rebecca Shelly's speech, which he credits with swinging the delegates over to the council idea (*Loose Leaves*, p. 172). Also see Lusk *Report*, I, 1045-1050, for the minutes of the meetings.

America was fighting a capitalistic war. The remaining sessions were quietly carried off under the eyes of a host of Justice Department agents who idly stood with their hands in their pockets.[42] Shortly after the conclusion of the rally, the Organizing Committee hurriedly began preparations to set up a national council movement. A permanent office was established at 2 West 13th Street, New York City, in the offices of the Emergency Peace Federation, and letters were sent to thousands of pacifists inviting them to attend the convention. The response to this appeal proved to be national. Thomas Van Lear, socialist mayor of Minneapolis, Senator John D. Works of California, Paul Jones, Episcopal bishop of Utah, Jacob Panken, New York socialist, Crystal Eastman, sister of Max, and Paul Kellogg, editor of the *Survey*, quickly reported their intentions to attend.[43]

Despite the increased pacifist interest in the council idea, David Starr Jordan had remained noncommittal. After leaving California for New York where he planned to investigate a new peace plan advocated by a group of Wall Street financiers, Jordan arrived in New York City prior to the Garden rally. The publicity given the Socialist party's role in this event disturbed Jordan to such an extent that he decided not to attend. He wrote his wife Jessie, "I will not join the Madison Square Garden discussions. While we often agree with socialists, often we don't."[44] Despite Jordan's refusal to appear at the Garden, he could not resist Lochner's constant requests for him to serve as treasurer of the Council until it could be organized nationally, and he agreed to serve until the Council was ready to elect a national treasurer.[45]

42. New York *Times*, June 1, 1917; First American Conference for Democracy and Terms of Peace, report, sixth session, May 31, 1917, Tamiment Institute. This same day Colonel House wrote Wilson: "The pacifists in this country, in England, and in Russia are demanding a statement of terms by the Allies which should declare against indemnities or territorial encroachment" (Baker, *Woodrow Wilson: Life and Letters*, VII, 96). The New York *Call*, June 1, 1917, declared that the council movement would "represent the unheard citizens of the nation" and would "demonstrate the strength of the socialist movement." For Max Eastman's reaction to the rally, see *Love and Revolution: My Journey Through an Epoch* (New York, 1964), p. 48.

43. First American Conference for Democracy and Terms of Peace, Organizing Committee for the Peoples Council of America, report, undated copy, Swarthmore Peace Collection. The Lusk *Report*, I, 1006.

44. Jordan to Jessie Jordan, May 31, 1917, Jordan papers.

45. Nominating Committee for the Peoples Council of America, report,

The Organizing Committee was not so fortunate in gaining the services of Jane Addams, who declined to join, although she was in sympathy with the idea. Numerous pleadings by both Lochner and Rebecca Shelly failed to change her mind.[46] Shortly thereafter, the committee approached Senator Robert M. La Follette of Wisconsin, but despite his daughter Fola's agreement to serve, the Senator remained sympathetic but not committed.[47]

As the Council pacifists spread their propaganda across the country, President Wilson became increasingly disturbed at the prospect that labor's anti-war radicals might seek to join with similar groups in England and France to form an international obstructionist movement.[48] Wilson sought the advice of his trusted aide, Colonel Edward House, who urged him to speak out against disloyalty before it became serious enough to disrupt the Administration's war policies. Wilson agreed and prepared to strike pacifism at home and abroad on June 14, Flag Day.[49]

But Wilson's speech did little to deter the anti-war movement. The following afternoon a delegation of Council pacifists led by Rabbi Magnes called at the White House to present the President the peace demands passed by the First American Conference for Democracy and Terms of Peace. The President's secretary, Joseph Tumulty, refused to accept either the delegation or its proposals. Undaunted, the group returned to New York and cabled their demands to the Kerenski government in Russia and to the British Labour party. At the same time the Organizing Committee ordered Job Harriman to set up a Council rally in San Francisco that

---

undated copy, Swarthmore Peace Collection; also Jordan to Comstock, Oct. 20, 1918, Jordan papers.

46. James W. Linn, *Jane Addams* (New York, 1930), p. 329; Lusk *Report*, I, 1060-1061.

47. La Follette was deeply interested in the Russian situation but stayed away from any clear-cut commitment to the council movement. See Belle Case La Follette and Fola La Follette, *Robert M. La Follette* (New York, 1953), II, 751-754.

48. Baker, *Woodrow Wilson: Life and Letters*, VII, 96; Aaron J. Levy to Tumulty, May 29, 1917, Lansing papers, Vol. 28; J. C. Koons to Lansing, May 31, 1917, Postmaster General's papers, Group 28, National Archives; Burleson to Lansing, June 1, 1917, *ibid.*

49. Baker, *Woodrow Wilson: Life and Letters*, VII, 97. On June 2, anti-war stickers began to appear in Chicago: "Workers refuse to murder and be murdered. Organize against autocracy at the place of production" (Burleson to Lansing, June 2, 1917, *ibid.*).

summer.[50] The prospects that the council movement would spread into the West alarmed Senator Sherman of Illinois, who called on Congress to stop this anti-war agitation by force if necessary.[51] But Congress was preoccupied with the necessities of war and paid little attention to these radicals as they made plans to hold a giant peace rally in Chicago during August.[52]

By June, 1917, neither Wilson's strong statements against pacifism nor the A.F. of L.'s support of the Administration had discouraged the council idea from spreading throughout the country.[53] But whatever success the anti-war radicals would have with their program would depend upon their arousing the worker to their cause.[54] That summer the pacifists and socialists hoped to build a strong anti-war labor movement capable of disrupting the war effort and challenging the loyal position of the A.F. of L.[55]

Chapter 3. The Federation Reacts to Pacifism

For several weeks following the opening of the Council's national organizing campaign, the A.F. of L. leadership paid little attention to labor radicalism. It was not long, however, before disturbing rumors were heard of the Council's success in organizing the

50. New York *Call*, June 5, 1917. Harriman, one of the founders of the Socialist party, was then residing in the Far West.

51. *Ibid.*, June 7, 1917.

52. *Ibid.*, June 12, 1917.

53. The International Workers of the World organizations were not asked to co-operate with the council movement; however, they corresponded from time to time with Council pacifists, and an individual I.W.W. member, also of the Council, sometimes spoke at a western rally along with various Council speakers. See Fred Thompson, *The I.W.W.: Its First Fifty Years* (Chicago, 1955), and William Preston, Jr., *Aliens and Dissenters: Federal Suppression of Radicals, 1903-1933* (Cambridge, 1963).

54. Scott Nearing, "The Peoples Council and What It Stands For," Nov., 1917, copy, Swarthmore Peace Collection; also Lusk *Report*, I, 1052, 1030-1038; Louis P. Lochner to author, Aug. 19, 1961.

55. Although the Socialist party co-operated in every way possible with the Council, the greatest obstacle to successful co-operation lay in the party's inability to supply the pacifists with money. Judge Jacob Panken, a leading New York City socialist who was prominent in the council movement, wrote: "The Party did not and could not finance the Peoples Council much as we wanted and the Council deserved. We had no surpluses, we were poor, depending from day to day on contributions from Party members" (Panken to author, Oct. 18, 1965).

anti-war Jewish immigrants in New York, especially those in the East Side garment industry. When several A.F. of L. officials complained to Gompers about this pacifist activity, he hurried to New York to confer with Central Federated Union leaders over the danger of obstructionism in the garment industry. Gompers soon learned that the council movement was not confined solely to New York but was spreading into the western portions of the nation. Realizing that the Council was a pacifist organization intent upon obstructing the war effort and challenging the A.F. of L.'s right to represent labor, Gompers and the local union men decided to form a counteragency. During June and July he met with these New York labor leaders and developed plans to stop the spread of the Council's anti-war propaganda.

Among those associates of Gompers who became alarmed lest the Council infiltrate the garment industry, which was then fulfilling orders for tents and uniforms, was pro-war socialist Robert Maisel, director of the National Labor Publicity Organization and formerly a member of the New York *Call*'s staff. Maisel had resigned from the socialist newspaper after the party's strong anti-war stand at St. Louis on April 7. But despite his resignation Maisel continued to maintain contact with many of his former associates, who supplied him from time to time with information concerning the future plans of the Council. Maisel learned that the Council planned to take over his N.L.P.O., which acted as a clearinghouse for labor publications in the New York area, so as to prevent the distribution of loyal labor material and facilitate the distribution of pacifist labor propaganda. By threatening to withdraw the business of a large number of socialist and pacifist labor organizations from his publicity organization, the Council hoped to pressure Maisel to co-operate or face financial ruin.[1] Because of his opposition to the Council, Maisel soon had lost so many of his customers that his agency was on the verge of bankruptcy. He hurriedly turned to Samuel Gompers and the A.F. of L. unions for aid before the N.L.P.O. could be forced out of business. Maisel reminded Gompers of the value of his agency to the orthodox labor movement and its usefulness in distributing loyal labor propaganda.[2]

1. Maisel to Gompers, June 9, 1917, Gompers papers.
2. *Ibid.*

Maisel's urgent requests for aid only confirmed Gompers' fears that the council movement was making good progress in the New York area. Although he had been keenly aware of the agitation of numerous pacifist labor organizations since 1914, he was deeply concerned over the prospect that the workingmen's council idea would influence the immigrants of the area. Gompers therefore encouraged Maisel to continue supplying him with news of the Council's activities: "Your letter concerning the situation among the so-called progressive unions in the New York City area was read with great interest. Keep me fully advised, I appreciate your cooperation."[3]

Encouraged by the prospect of obtaining additional business from the loyal labor unions, Maisel frequently supplied Gompers with confidential information concerning the Council's activities. One bit of news was especially interesting. At a secret meeting held in Morris Hillquit's office, three editors of the foremost socialist publications, the *Jewish Daily Forward*, the New York *Call*, and the German language paper *Volkszeitung*, pledged their monetary support to the council movement and their columns to its anti-war propaganda. He also learned that the radicals were working to obtain control of the New York City unions before launching their national peace program. As Maisel aptly summed up the situation, "I believe that it is a fight to the finish."[4]

The Council's plan to control the New York area unions focused on the Central Federated Union, an organization which united the vast majority of the city's workers. The C.F.U.'s secretary, Ernest Bohm, had long managed to hold control of that organization against the most determined opponents of his conservatism. Yet the situation became serious when the Council made an all-out effort in June to wrest the C.F.U. from Bohm's control. The method used was a familiar one in socialist circles. Anti-war radicals were first to gain control of their local unions and then send delegates to the C.F.U. where they were to seize control of

3. Gompers to Maisel, June 10, 1917, Gompers copy books.
4. Taft, *The A.F. of L. in the Time of Gompers*, p. 181. The dispute among Gompers, the United Hebrew Trades, and the *Forward* goes back to 1915 when these agencies were critical of Gompers' pro-war stand. For a short history of the Trades, see H. Lang and C. Feinstone, *Gewerkschaften* (New York, 1938), copy in the Jewish Archives of the New York Public Library.

that federation's top offices. This threat alarmed many of New York's moderate labor leaders who, like Gompers, had begun to receive repeated reports of the Council's intentions. Hugh Frayne, who was on an A.F. of L. mission in the New York area, appealed to Gompers to "open fire against them [pacifists] immediately,"[5] and Maisel warned that the Socialist party was behind the Council's programs.[6] Alarmed at this pacifist and socialist alliance, Gompers planned to appear before the C.F.U.'s Executive Committee and impress upon them the need for an organized opposition to the radicals.[7]

While Gompers prepared his New York trip, the press in that area had learned of the Council's plans to take over the local unions. The New York *Times* led a verbal assault on what it termed the "pro-German activities" of the Council by publishing reports that the group was financed with German money and was working to spread obstructionism throughout the country. The *Times* editor warned the radicals, "We know that the Federal Government is watching this closely."[8] Coinciding with the *Times's* attack upon the Council, other publications had high praise for Gompers' determination to stop the movement. The New York *Analyst* proclaimed that Gompers was not "the radical of old" who had defied the government but was now "working hand in hand with the Wilson Administration to make the A.F. of L. the most democratic labor Federation in the country."[9]

During this newspaper exposé of the council movement, Gompers asked the C.F.U. Executive Committee to meet with

5. Hugh Frayne to Gompers, June 12, 1917, Gompers papers.

6. Maisel to Gompers, June 26, 1917, *ibid.* Maisel wrote that "Hillquit is playing first fiddle" in the Council.

7. At this time Gompers and Secretary of War Newton D. Baker were discussing ways to keep down labor unrest in the war plants (Baker, *Woodrow Wilson: Life and Letters,* VII, 120).

8. New York *Times,* June 21, 1917. The government was also trying to contain Jewish unrest. On June 29 Rabbi Stephen S. Wise consulted with Wilson about a plan to create an American Jewish Congress to unite the various Jewish elements behind the war effort. Wilson heartily approved (Baker, *Woodrow Wilson: Life and Letters,* VII, 135). The government looked upon the council movement much as Christopher Lasch describes: "A Soviet movement which was the most immediate and tangible manifestation in America of the Russian Revolution" (*The American Liberals and the Russian Revolution* [New York, 1962], p. 40).

9. *Analyst* (New York), June 18, 1917.

him at the Continental Hotel for a discussion of radicalism in the New York area.[10] For several hours he urged the committee to work with him to resist the pacifist propaganda being spread by the Council and to back the A.F. of L.'s position of supporting the war until Germany was totally defeated.[11] Because most of those present agreed with Gompers that obstructionism would do the labor movement no good, Bohm promised that he would present Gompers' suggestions before the next general meeting of the C.F.U. After the local papers' exposé of the Council as an obstructionist movement, Bohm was anxious for the C.F.U. to remain loyal, and he later promised Gompers, "They [the pacifists] will know that they have been in a battle."[12] Meanwhile, Gompers returned to Washington and waited for word that the C.F.U. would co-operate with the A.F. of L.'s loyalty work in New York. On July 3 word arrived from Bohm that "although the pot is boiling the C.F.U. will support the A.F. of L.'s proposals." The rank-and-file, he related, "fully agree with your statements made at the meeting before the Central on June 29 to Americanize the labor movement in greater New York."[13]

With the C.F.U.'s support assured, Gompers watched the Council's activities in New York to anticipate their next move. Reports came in weekly, particularly from Maisel, who estimated the real strength of the movement. The Council, he reported, was dispatching dozens of organizers into the New York area and paying them high salaries. At the same time, the pacifists were mailing from six to seven hundred invitations weekly to numerous anti-war groups to join the council movement.[14] Impressed by this activity, Gompers made several trips to New York to formulate plans for loyalty work in that area. Prodded on by Maisel who warned, "There is no blinking at their size," Gompers and Bohm

10. Gompers to Benjamin Schlesinger, June 27, 1917, Gompers copy books.
11. Gompers, *Seventy Years*, II, 380-381. Gompers criticized the Jewish members of the Central Federated Union for not backing the war effort, and he warned them that they could be called traitors for their anti-war stand. See *Miller's Weekly*, editorial, July 6, 1917.
12. Ernest Bohm to Gompers, confidential memorandum, July 2, 1917, Gompers papers.
13. Bohm to Gompers, July 3, 1917, *ibid*.
14. Maisel to Gompers, memorandum, undated copy in *ibid*.

hurriedly organized plans for an agency that would devote its entire time to countering the pacifist propaganda of the Council.[15] By the latter part of July, they had completed arrangements for the C.F.U. to co-operate with the A.F. of L. in setting up such an organization in New York City. The new agency was to be called the American Alliance for Labor and Democracy and was to welcome any laborer who wished to support the war effort and labor conservatism.

Since the Alliance was publicized as welcoming any pro-war supporter, J. G. Phelps Stokes and John Spargo, the leaders of the pro-war socialist faction which had bolted the party in St. Louis, were deeply interested. For some time both men had been searching for a way to co-operate with the war effort without sacrificing their socialist principles.[16] But to remain within the party and serve with Hillquit, Berger, and Debs was out of the question, for there was no indication at this time that they would ever support the war effort. Consequently, Spargo resigned from the party on June 1. In July Stokes, who had attempted to work within the party, also resigned.[17] Stokes followed the formation of the American Alliance for Labor and Democracy with interest and informed Chester Wright, who had resigned from the staff of the New York *Call* for similar reasons, of his desire to be with the Alliance. Stokes implied that he favored "Gompers' stand on the war issue."[18] The Alliance soon attracted Spargo, Walling, Rus-

15. Central Federated Union minutes, Continental Hotel, July 21, 1917, copy in *ibid*.

16. T. D. Seymour Bassett to author, Dec. 12, 1962. Bassett recalls that Spargo once said that President Wilson talked with him about joining in the effort to support loyalty work. On July 17 Wilson wrote: "Indeed I have seen very many evidences of late that the bulk of the socialists in this country have genuine American feelings and in no sense represent the revolutionary temper such as Mr. Berger has shown" (Baker, *Woodrow Wilson: Life and Letters*, VII, 170).

17. At this time Stokes appears to have been undecided about his relationship with his former friends. He criticized the State Department for refusing to allow Hillquit, Lee, Maurer, and Berger passports to Stockholm (New York *Call*, July 10, 1917). Earlier in May he had denied that the the pro-war socialists were in any way connected with the anti-war faction (Stokes to *American Socialist Magazine*, May 28, 1917, copy in Socialist Party papers, No. 16, Duke University).

18. Stokes to Chester Wright, July 12, 1917, J. G. Phelps Stokes papers, Box 27, Butler Library, Columbia University, New York City.

sell, and numerous other pro-war socialists who, like Stokes, wished to co-operate with the war effort.[19]

Hearing through Maisel that these pro-war socialists were interested in joining the Alliance, Gompers realized that this was a golden opportunity to facilitate the schism in the socialists' ranks by carrying off part of the party's intelligentsia. He ordered Maisel to meet with the pro-war socialists in the Continental Hotel on the evening of July 28 and work out some basis for their co-operation. Spargo and Stokes quickly accepted. Stokes was impressed by the Alliance because it planned to accept any pro-war radical, and he enthusiastically informed Spargo, "From what Maisel tells me the possibilities are immense."[20]

The Continental Hotel meeting was well attended by representatives of the A.F. of L. and the pro-war socialists. A committee composed of socialists Spargo, Chester Wright, and several Jewish editors worked with Frank Morrison, Hugh Frayne, and Ernest Bohm of the A.F. of L. to lay out the framework for an agreement which incorporated into the Alliance any socialist who favored a moderate approach to labor's problems.[21] Hearing that his pro-war friends in the East were joining the Alliance, W. R. Gaylord of Wisconsin quickly offered his services.[22]

The pro-war socialists' interest in the Alliance appeared to be a triumph for the A.F. of L.; but nothing could have been further from the truth. Although Gompers counted it a success in gaining the support of these party intellectuals, Stokes and Spargo had their reasons for co-operating. Both men carried on a remarkable correspondence in which they discussed plans to create a dual socialist movement while, at the same time, co-operating with the Alliance: through their association with the A.F. of L. they planned to build a loyal socialist movement. Even as Stokes had written Chester Wright of his support for the A.F. of L.'s loyalty work, he had also dispatched a second letter to a friend, C. E. Fleet, declaring his and Spargo's intentions to set up a new social-

19. Bell, "Background and Development," pp. 312-313.
20. Stokes to Spargo, July 25, 1917, Stokes papers, Box 27. Spargo informed Stokes that the Alliance must not be too closely tied to the A.F. of L., or the pro-war socialists would tend to shy away (Spargo to Stokes, July 30, 1917, copy, Gompers papers).
21. Maisel to Stokes, Aug. 2, 1917, Stokes papers, Box 27.
22. Gaylord to Stokes, Aug. 17, 1917, *ibid.*

ist party which would materialize "within a few months."[23] The movement would be headed by themselves and would be a "League of all pro-war socialists who wished to support the war effort."[24] The idea of a dual movement had occurred earlier to Stokes and Spargo, and both had discussed it seriously since June, 1917.[25] The decision to co-operate with the A.F. of L. Alliance was an attempt to use loyal labor's support to further the cause of a loyal socialist movement; or as Stokes put it, "I have no doubt that there are certain people who are trying to use us. I see no reason however why we should not, in this incident, reciprocate. . . ."[26] Spargo had been thinking along similar lines: "I know as well as you do, or, for that matter, as well as any man can—that Gompers is playing a deep game of his own." He slyly boasted, "I am confident that I can out play my old friend." Spargo advised his followers to take advantage of their co-operation with the Alliance to "get in close to the average labor union man."[27] Stokes echoed the same idea when he pointed out that supporting Gompers was "an added bond" to attract respectable people to a dual socialist movement.[28]

While Stokes and Spargo worked to build their own movement, the Alliance elected its permanent officers. Frank Morrison, secretary of the A.F. of L., became temporary chairman; the important post of director went to Maisel, partially as a reward for his faithful service and partially because he had made a perfect liaison between the Alliance and the pro-war socialists. The Advisory Council included Spargo, Russell, and Walling, but it was weighted with A.F. of L. men: Ernest Bohm, James P. Holland, an A.F. of L. organizer, W. E. Small of the Typographic Union, Hugh Frayne, and David J. Berry of the National Labor *Journal*.[29]

23. Stokes to C. E. Fleet, July 12, 1917, *ibid.*
24. Stokes to Spargo, July 17, 1917, *ibid.*
25. Spargo to F. C. Pitts, July 18, 1917, copy in *ibid.*
26. Stokes to Spargo, Aug. 21, 1917, *ibid.*
27. Spargo to B. C. Marsh, Aug. 21, 1917, copy in *ibid.* The dual movement advocated by Spargo eventually became the National party.
28. Stokes to Lewis Wallis, Aug. 21, 1917, *ibid.* Spargo later wrote that "A man can simultaneously be both a good socialist and a good American" (*America and Social Democracy* [New York, 1918], pp. 35, 109).
29. Executive Conference, minutes, American Alliance, July 29, 1917, copy, Gompers papers.

Of immense importance was Frank P. Walsh's later decision to join the movement along with Chester Wright, who joined the Alliance's propaganda staff. The officers quickly approved a pledge of loyalty "to stand unreservedly by the ideals of the Republic in stress or in storm" and opened their headquarters in the offices of Maisel's N.L.P.O. at 51 Chambers Street.[30]

Shortly thereafter Maisel dramatically announced that the Committee on Public Information would finance the Alliance's program.[31] The C.P.I.'s acceptance of the Alliance as a member agency was the result of the Administration's realization that the country's skilled workers must be kept behind the war effort. For after America entered the war, Wilson had become increasingly concerned over the possibility that labor's anti-war elements might disrupt the war effort by strikes and sabotage.[32] Indeed, the President had sought the co-operation of the A.F. of L. as early as 1916 when he appointed Gompers a member of the Advisory Commission of the Council of National Defense. Consequently, the A.F. of L. maintained contacts with the government's highest echelons. Not only could Gompers approach the President if the occasion warranted, but Secretary of Labor William B. Wilson, a former mineworker, listened sympathetically to the Federation's problems. By appointing Gompers to the C.N.D., Wilson had shown his willingness to work closely with the A.F. of L. in solving the country's wartime labor problems.[33]

Realizing the importance of the A.F. of L. to the President, Gompers had been working to co-ordinate the Federation's wartime policies with those of the government. In this, he usually received the fullest co-operation of both the President and the Secretary of Labor.[34] Because of the A.F. of L.'s willingness to

30. Wright to Gompers, Aug. 4, 1917, *ibid.*

31. New York *Times*, July 30, 1917; Executive Conference, minutes, American Alliance, July 29, 1917, Gompers papers.

32. Baker, *Woodrow Wilson: Life and Letters*, VII, 190.

33. Clarkson, *Industrial America and the War*, pp. 91-92.

34. John Lombardi, *Labor's Voice in the Cabinet: The History of the Department of Labor from Its Origin to 1921* (New York, 1942), p. 180. "President Gompers of the A.F. of L. was given every encouragement by the Administration to rally labor to a preparedness program and to wean it away from pacifist and radical influences. . . . He became a frequent visitor to the White House where he was consulted by the President on labor union matters here and abroad" (p. 205).

support the government during the critical period of 1915 and 1916, the Federation's prestige had risen to a high point.[35] In turn, Gompers used his influence with the government to push the Federation's reform programs. As long as the A.F. of L. held the confidence of the government, it was strongly resistant to obstructionism.[36] Its pleas did not fall on deaf ears; the C.N.D. and the Department of Labor had been concerned with the causes of industrial unrest since early 1917.[37] On July 12 Gompers spoke before the C.N.D. on the importance of the laborer to the war effort, and the next day Secretary Baker appealed to President Wilson to listen sympathetically to the A.F. of L.'s demands for better working conditions in the war plants.[38]

It is not clear just when the Administration decided to take a direct hand in aiding the A.F. of L. in its opposition to labor disloyalty, but by July 26 Wilson had made his decision to support the New York Alliance and help it expand into a national organization. Creel advised Gompers of the good news: "I am ready to get behind you and the Central Federated Union in your attempt to Americanize the labor movement. Out of my knowledge of you and the men associated with you I have the conviction that it is not necessary to explain such efforts. In order to have this, all support must be open and above board."[39] Gompers himself sheds little light on the decision, saying simply in his autobiography that he presented the C.N.D. with his loyalty program and then talked with Creel about it. He admitted at the time that neither the A.F. of L. rank-and-file nor the Administration had given the Executive Committee any prior authority to organize the Alliance.[40] Nevertheless, the deed was done and the newly formed Alliance was to be the financial responsibility of the C.P.I.

35. *Ibid.*, pp. 206-207.

36. David Cronon, ed., *The Cabinet Diaries of Josephus Daniels, 1913-1921* (Lincoln, Neb., 1963), p. 164.

37. Lombardi, *Labor's Voice in the Cabinet*, "Wartime Activities," pp. 173-204.

38. Frederick Palmer, *Newton D. Baker, American at War* (New York, 1931). "Perhaps the wisest action of the Council of National Defense, when it appointed an Advisory Commission of industrial experts, had been to make Samuel Gompers, President of the American Federation of Labor, the member of labor" (I, 259).

39. Creel to Gompers, July 26, 1917, Committee on Public Information papers, I-A1-17, National Archives, Washington, D.C.

40. Gompers, *Seventy Years*, II, 382.

Maisel was ordered to submit his propaganda requisitions to C. D. Lee of the C.P.I.'s Division of Business Management with the notation, "Please order for the Division of the American Alliance for Labor and Democracy."[41] Salaries, rents, and other payments were to be submitted likewise.

Shortly after the C.P.I. accepted the Alliance as its labor propaganda agency, Maisel began plans to spread loyalty propaganda throughout the country. That most critical of all items, money, seemed no longer to be a problem. His first action was to have printed several thousand copies of "The Purposes and Principles of the American Alliance For Labor and Democracy," which explained the program set forth on July 28 at the Continental Hotel.[42] The "Purposes and Principles" pointed out that every workingman was expected to support his government "in carrying the present war for justice, freedom and democracy to a triumphant conclusion . . . ," and that "disloyalty to America in this crisis is disloyalty to the cause of freedom, democracy and internationalism." Members were told, "Not even at the bequest of the so-called Peoples Council will the organized workers of America prostitute the labor movement to serve the brutal power responsible for the infamous rape of Belgium—the power that would subject Russia to a worse despotism than that of the Romanoffs."[43] Next, Maisel urged Gompers to become the permanent chairman and Spargo to become the first vice-president. With the A.F. of L. behind the movement and with federal money at its disposal, the Alliance hoped to counter the propaganda of the Peoples Council of America.[44]

41. Mock and Larson, *Words That Won the War*, p. 189. Creel largely ignores the Alliance's role within the C.P.I. framework. For the largest single collection of Alliance-C.P.I. correspondence, see the Gompers papers and the C.P.I. papers, I-A5 and A6.

42. "Purposes and Principles of the American Alliance for Labor and Democracy," copy, Gompers papers.

43. *Ibid.*, pp. 4, 5, 8.

44. Spargo's membership card is with his papers in the library of the University of Vermont. On August 15, 1917, Gompers sent out a circular to all unions urging them to support the Alliance (copy, Gompers papers). Some historians have been suspicious of the Alliance's spontaneity, hinting that it was established by the Wilson Administration for the labor movement. See Austin Van Der Slice, *International Labor, Diplomacy and Peace* (Philadelphia, 1941), p. 270; James H. Maurer, *It Can Be Done* (New York, 1938), pp. 221, 227-228; James O'Neal, "The Socialist in the War," *American Mercury* (April, 1927), pp. 418-426. J. G. Phelps Stokes,

Gompers, who had for some weeks attacked the Stockholm peace propaganda being spread by the anti-war radicals,[45] ordered the Alliance to print propaganda promising the worker untold benefits if he co-operated with his government. "The new days of fuller freedom, equality, justice, social and economic readjustment are to overflow from this terrible crucible of war," he said; but labor must first "prove its merits to play a principle role in the human drama of tomorrow," then, "Out of this will arise the golden days for the men who toil."[46] Additional propaganda was printed stressing the workers' importance in backing up their "brothers" at the front lines.[47] In this way, Alliance propaganda began to roll from the C.P.I.'s presses, financed by federal funds, distributed under the name of the American Alliance For Labor and Democracy, sponsored by the A. F. of L. Executive Committee, and supported by the pro-war socialists.

But the Alliance had much organizing to do before it could compete with the fast-moving Peoples Council. By early June, Lochner and his Organizing Committee had added to their ranks Professor L. M. Keasbey of the University of Texas. Scott Nearing was placed in charge of infiltrating the A.F. of L. unions by directing the campaigns of those anti-war radicals bent on running for office. Plans were completed to have David Starr Jordan go to Washington, D.C., and gain the support of those congressmen eager to attack the Wilson Administration. Jordan, who was in New York City, agreed to co-operate because he believed he could impress the need for a negotiated peace upon Wilson's critics.[48] While gaining Jordan's co-operation, Lochner once again prepared to urge Frank P. Walsh to join the Council. Job Harriman was to act as intermediary between Lochner and Walsh; and if this failed, Professor Keasbey was to be sent along with Hillquit

however, shortly before his death denied that the Wilson Administration had urged Gompers to create the Alliance. Although admitting that "conversations were held with people in high standing," Stokes declared the Alliance to have been spontaneous (Stokes to author, Feb. 11, 1960).

45. "This is no time for the working people of the Allies to gather in a peace conference the action of which might hamper the efficiency of the nation's fighting forces," he had said (New York *Times*, Aug. 5, 1917).

46. "Up America and At 'Em," A.A.L.D. publication, Gompers papers.

47. "Carrying on the Fight at Home," *ibid.*

48. Organizing Committee minutes, P.C.A., fifth session, June 8, 1917, Swarthmore; Lusk *Report*, I, 1052-1054.

and Harriman to gain Walsh's support. But Wilson had just appointed Walsh to the War Labor Board, a position which Walsh desired and one in which he hoped to work for the benefit of labor. On June 20 he again refused to serve with Lochner.[49] Jordan arrived in Washington and started a round of discussions, causing Lochner humorously to refer to him as a "schoolmaster to the would-be statesmen."[50] Nevertheless, Lochner had confidence in Jordan's ability to convert Wilson's critics to pacifism: "I feel certain that we shall soon command a tremendous strength not only morally, but politically. . . ."[51] He believed that there was an excellent chance that Jordan might persuade Senators Borah, Hiram Johnson, and George Norris to co-operate in a limited way with the Council.[52] An amusing side line to Jordan's lobbying in Washington came to light when a former Confederate veteran who had been reading of the Council's opposition to the Administration sent Rebecca Shelly a list of Democratic party members who he believed would be interested in aiding the movement because it seemed to be opposing the growing power of the federal government.[53]

Although Jordan's efforts to rally pacifist support in Congress were inconclusive, Lochner went ahead with his organizing work. As a first step, he set up a propaganda printing press in the offices of the Emergency Peace Federation at 2 West 13th Street; with this action, the E.P.F. ceased to exist as a separate body and became incorporated into the Peoples Council.[54] Lochner also asked Job Harriman, who wished to return to his communal work in the Far West, to organize support for the Council in California, and Eugene Debs, who had recently joined the movement, to aid with organizational work in the Midwest.[55] The Executive Com-

49. Lochner to Walsh, June 6, 14, 1917, Walsh papers, No. 16. Wilson's appointment of Walsh to the new War Labor Board was called "A masterful touch of a great politician" by H. L. Fagin of Houston, Texas (Fagin to Walsh, June 16, 1917, *ibid.*). Walsh again declined to serve the Council on June 20 (Walsh to Lochner, June 20, 1917, *ibid.*).

50. Lochner to Jordan, June 9, 1917, Jordan papers.

51. *Ibid.*

52. Jordan, *Days of a Man*, II, 740; Lusk *Report*, I, 1052-1053.

53. Shelly to Jordan, June 16, 1917, Jordan papers.

54. Organizing Committee minutes, P.C.A., seventh session, June 13, 1917, Swarthmore; Lusk *Report*, I, 1030.

55. Harriman was involved with the Llano colony at this time. See

mittee also elected its permanent officers. To no one's surprise, Lochner retained the post of general secretary; Lella Faye Secor, formerly of the Emergency Peace Federation, became organizing secretary; Rebecca Shelly, financial secretary; Elizabeth Freeman, legislative secretary; Scott Nearing, labor organizer; and Morris Hillquit, director. David Starr Jordan and H. W. L. Dana were asked to work with the Committee on International Cooperation, a field in which they both excelled.[56]

The newly elected officers set about deciding where to hold their national convention.[57] New York City was mentioned, but the East was proving to be less tolerant than the radicals had previously supposed. By June the C.F.U., under the prodding of Ernest Bohm, had begun to resist effectively the Council's efforts to take over the New York unions. There also had been a sharp increase in the area's newspaper attacks on the movement. As a result of these reversals, Hillquit, fearing that further notoriety might severely damage the Council's chances of success, suggested that the organization select for its convention site a midwestern city which contained a vigorous labor movement.[58]

The recent unfavorable publicity given the council movement in the New York area presented Rabbi Magnes with the opportunity to suggest that the organization stop trying to appeal primarily to the nation's extremists but to the needs of the ordinary laborer and farmer who desired only a higher standard of living. Referring to a recent report from the West by Job Harriman, Magnes pointed out that sympathy there for the council movement was strong, but it was primarily among non-socialist farmer groups. Further, he pointed out that support for the Council in Seattle was reported by Harriman to be slight because the people there distrusted the extreme position often taken by the movement. Magnes joined with Hillquit in suggesting that the Council pick a

Paul K. Conkin, *Two Paths to Utopia: The Hutterites and Llano Colony* (Lincoln, Neb., 1964).

56. Political Committee report, P.C.A., June 13, 1917, Swarthmore. "The possibilities of this movement are so tremendous that I would earnestly plead with you to set aside six Thursdays for the work of the Organizing Committee" (Lochner to Organizing Committee, June 19, 1917, copy in W. I. Hull papers, Swarthmore).

57. Political Committee report, P.C.A., June 13, 1917, Swarthmore.

58. Organizing Committee report, P.C.A., eighth session, June 15, 1917, *ibid.*; Hillquit, *Loose Leaves*, p. 173.

western city for the convention, but he strongly urged that the organization's program be toned down.[59] It was difficult to build a moderate image for the Council when it continued to add socialists such as John Reed and Max Pine, secretary of the United Hebrew Trades, to its roster.[60] Despite a New York *Call* editorial emphasizing that membership in the newly forming Council committed no one to socialism, the suspicion lingered that the council movement was primarily a socialistic adventure.[61] At the same time, the Council itself refused to repudiate its close association with the Socialist party and, indeed, asked the party to donate the month of July exclusively to the distribution of Council propaganda.[62] Despite the close co-operation between the pacifists and the socialists, there is no evidence that the Council was financed by the Socialist party. Nor is there any indication that the Council's declaration—"We have no endowment or source of income. We depend solely upon voluntary contributions"—was not absolutely correct.[63] Its close co-operation with the Socialist party, however, often made it appear that the Council was a wing of that organization.[64]

Despite a constant lack of funds, the Council managed to operate on a shoestring, an ideal, and much voluntary labor. It was all of these which finally launched the first of their midwestern peace rallies in Chicago. The Council pacifists hoped that this event would be as successful as the New York rally in May. The Chicago meeting started on July 7 in conjunction with the Chicago Peace Convention of the Socialist party. The White Sox baseball park had been chosen, but the notoriety of the event forced the

59. Organizing Committee report, P.C.A., ninth session, June 20, 1917, *ibid.*

60. New York *Call*, June 20, 1917.

61. The New York *Call*, June 23, 1917, reported that Max Pine, secretary of the United Hebrew Trades, would help organize a socialist labor wing of the Peoples Council.

62. Financial Committee report, P.C.A., June 21, 1917, Swarthmore.

63. P.C.A. publication, undated copy, *ibid.*

64. Attempts to have the Justice Department open its F.B.I. files on several investigations of the council movement have failed (S. A. Andretta to author, Feb. 16, 1961). A search of the financial statements of the Socialist party, 1917-1918, at Duke University, and the remaining financial papers of the Council located in the Tamiment Institute, show no contributions by the party to the Council. The Council never had more than $30,000 on hand at any one time.

pacifists into the Riverview picnic grounds.[65] As usual, Justice Department agents were present and the crowd was patrolled by a strong contingent of local police. Senator William E. Mason of Illinois was the foremost of twelve speakers who urged the crowd of five thousand to accept the Bolshevik peace proposals as the only solution for a just peace. But the rally was only a partial success. Jane Addams had refused to attend, there had been some scuffling between the pacifists and several onlookers, and the newspapers in Chicago had billed the gathering as "socialistic" and "pro-German."[66] Lochner was enthusiastic over the rally, but Maisel, observing the event for the Alliance, wrote back to Gompers, "The convention was a bust!"[67] Lochner, however, followed up the Chicago rally by sending organizers into St. Louis, Kansas City, and Salt Lake City; while Council organizers on the West Coast laid the groundwork for similar rallies in Los Angeles, July 20; San Francisco, July 22; and Philadelphia, July 25, 1917.[68]

The Los Angeles rally was planned by former Senator John Works of California, who had failed to gain re-election, and Elizabeth Freeman, who had traveled west to work with him on the project.[69] Lochner asked Jordan to speak at this rally,[70] but Jordan had read of the notoriety surrounding the Chicago meeting and refused, despite Lochner's constant pleadings.[71] Jordan did, however, send the Council his best wishes for a successful confer-

65. New York *Times*, July 8, 1917. James Maurer was in Chicago helping to organize the rally (New York *Call*, July 7, 1917).

66. New York *Times*, July 9, 1917. The Post Office Department had obtained some of the Council's propaganda concerning the Chicago rally and had turned it over to the Justice Department (Koones to Lansing, July 6, 1917, Postmaster General's papers).

67. Maisel to Gompers, July 11, 1917, Gompers papers.

68. Lochner had stated in the New York *Call*, July 12, 1917, that more than eight thousand persons had attended the Chicago rally, not two thousand as stated by the New York *Times*. Lochner declared that the original site for the meetings had been "mysteriously denied" the Council (Organizing Committee report, P.C.A., twelfth session, July 12, 1917, Swarthmore).

69. Lusk *Report*, I, 1063. Works was also planning to speak at the San Francisco rally. "I have for some time been preparing with a great deal of care a formal address to be delivered at the meeting to be held in San Francisco" (Works to Lochner, June 27, 1917, copy, Swarthmore).

70. Lochner to Jordan, July 17, 1917, Jordan papers.

71. *Ibid.*

ence.[72] The Los Angeles rally was attended by approximately two hundred delegates and four hundred members from the local chapter. James Maurer and Works keynoted the event by praising the workingmen's councils of socialist Russia as democratic organizations whose counterparts would sweep the United States. Works also attacked the Wilson Administration for controlling the press and curtailing free speech, while Maurer told of the A.F. of L.'s success in pressuring the Pennsylvania state legislature not to pass labor legislation desired by the socialists.[73] These accusations were commented upon by the local press which accused the pacifists of agitating to disrupt the West Coast's war industry.

After reading of this further notoriety, Jordan hurriedly sent his resignation to the Council. But Lochner only reacted by pointing out to Jordan that his resignation would do untold harm to the council movement at this natal stage. He pleaded with Jordan to remain in the organization until its national convention: "I promise that by September when we turn over our jobs to the convention I will stop any attempt to re-elect you." Lochner admitted that the Los Angeles rally was "ill planned, although the results were rewarding."[74] But Jordan did not soften and the next day insisted upon resigning. Again Lochner pleaded with him not to desert the movement at this critical point, and Jordan, finally worn down by these persistent arguments, agreed to remain as the treasurer of the Council, but only until the national convention in September.[75]

The failure of the Los Angeles rally to attract favorable publicity on the West Coast was balanced by a successful rally in Philadelphia at the same time. More than 25,000 workers gathered to hear Hillquit promise that the Socialist party would give "The

72. New York *Call,* July 21, 1917. Jordan had been receiving poison-pen letters from those who were shocked that he had allowed his name to be associated with the Council (H. H. Barish to Jordan, June 26, 1917, Jordan papers). Rebecca Shelly also had received several of these letters and apparently passed them on to Jordan (copies in *ibid.*).

73. New York *Call,* July 20, 1917. Lochner told Jordan that the West Coast was "a most critical area" for the Council (Lochner to Jordan, July 17, 1917, *ibid.*).

74. Lochner to Jordan, Aug. 6, 1917, *ibid.*

75. Jordan to Lochner, telegram, Aug. 7, 1917; Lochner to Jordan, Aug. 8, 1917, *ibid.*

fullest possible cooperation to the Peoples Council"; while Nearing denounced the European war as a "capitalistic adventure"; and Norman Thomas attacked the draft and praised the conscientious objector. Not to be outdone by the others, Jacob Panken accused the A.F. of L. for selling out to the government and Gompers for "throwing himself into the war back in 1914 even before the United States had entered."[76]

On the West Coast the San Francisco rally of August 8 was to have made up for the poor showing demonstrated at the Los Angeles rally, but the meeting went badly for the Council speakers. Confident that their national membership would soon reach 1,800,000, the speakers prepared a severe attack on the Wilson Administration. Standing nearby was a contingent of Justice Department agents and local police watchfully waiting for any hint of seditious intent. They did not wait long, for several remarks made by the city attorney, Daniel O'Connell, in a sharp speech attacking conscription were interpreted as seditious and O'Connell was promptly arrested. Incensed by this action, former Senator Works called the arrest "an attempt by the Wilson Administration to intimidate thinking people."[77]

The arrest of O'Connell greatly upset Jordan who had become increasingly disturbed at the alarming number of reckless statements being made by the Council's speakers. ("As is usual in similar groupings the extremists ran away with the organization," he was later to write).[78] Once again he wrote Lochner that his name must be dropped from the Council's lists if any further embarrassing incidents occurred. Jordan concluded, "I must be custodian of my own shadow."[79] He had been concerned about several earlier incidents. Professor Keasbey of the University of Texas was dismissed for his work on the Council's behalf, and

76. New York *Call*, July 15, 22, 1917.
77. P.C.A. *Bulletin*, Vol. I, No. 1, Aug. 7, 1917, Swarthmore; New York *Times*, Aug. 9, 1917.
78. Jordan, *Days of a Man*, II, 738-739; also R. L. Wilbur to Jordan, July 24, 1917, Jordan papers. An I.W.W. official spoke with the Council at San Francisco (Lusk *Report*, I, 1068).
79. Jordan to Lochner, Aug. 26, 1917, Jordan papers. Lochner later played down his attempts to bring Jordan into the council movement (Lochner to author, Aug. 19, 1961).

Keasbey attracted further notoriety by agreeing to become a Council organizer in the Texas area.[80]

Other incidents had occurred. Lochner had ordered Isaac McBride, a former secretary to Senator Lane of Oregon, to arrange a meeting for the Council with members of Senator George F. Chamberlain's Military Affairs Committee.[81] Lochner believed that the committee might be willing to listen to Senator Lane's former secretary.[82] At the same time the Council had decided to communicate with the socialist members of the German Reichstag concerning Germany's war aims.[83] On July 23 the Council had sent an appeal to Secretary of State Lansing requesting him to clear a cablegram to these socialists.[84] Neither President Wilson nor Lansing had any intention of permitting the Council to communicate directly with the German socialists, and the government flatly refused to permit the communication.[85] Rebuked by the Administration, the Council had sought to reap propaganda value out of the incident by using the socialist press to attack the Administration.[86]

In the meantime, McBride had been busily arranging for a delegation of Council officials to appear before Senator Chamberlain.[87] He had gained a hearing on August 7 before "a committee of friendly Congressmen."[88] The Council delegation led by McBride, Lochner, Max Eastman, and H. W. L. Dana had appeared before Senators Henry of Arkansas, Gronner of North Dakota, Owen of Oklahoma, Rankin of Montana, Jones of Wash-

80. New York *Times*, July 21, 1917; Organizing Committee report, P.C.A., July 19, 1917, Swarthmore. Lansing had just spoken out against pacifism in his Madison Barracks speech. He received dozens of letters congratulating him for attacking "These evil and presistant [*sic*] efforts exerted to divide American loyalty and duty . . ." (William Feitelbaum to Lansing, July 30, 1917, Lansing papers, No. 29).

81. Organizing Committee report, P.C.A., twelth session, July 12, 1917, Swarthmore.

82. Lochner to McBride, July 13, 1917, Swarthmore; New York *Call*, July 28, 1917.

83. P.C.A. press release, July 19, 1917, Swarthmore.

84. New York *Call*, July 30, 1917.

85. New York *Times*, July 30, 1917.

86. Organizing Committee report, P.C.A., fourteenth session, July 26, 1917, Swarthmore.

87. *Ibid.*

88. Organizing Committee report, P.C.A., sixteenth session, Aug. 7, 1917, *ibid.*

ington, Johnson of California, Lindenbery of Minnesota, and Chamberlain.[89] But the meeting had not gone smoothly; when the pacifists failed to persuade the senators of the importance of a negotiated peace based on the Bolsheviks' terms, they turned to haranguing the legislators with their views on labor, censorship, and America's war aims.[90] The meeting only resulted in further bad publicity for the Council.

Disappointed at their failure to persuade the senators of the need for a negotiated peace, the group had gone to Senator Robert La Follette and had urged him to introduce his own peace plan. La Follette introduced a plan before the Senate, but Senator King of Utah, infuriated that a pacifist such as La Follette dared advise the Administration on its policies, had introduced a resolution asking that La Follette be censured for his "pro-German" attitude. This had touched off a vigorous debate, but after tempers had cooled, neither the La Follette peace proposal nor King's resolution had been seriously considered by the Senate.[91]

The notoriety of the council movement had increased during July and August. With each peace rally, Council speakers had become more forthright in their demands for an end to the war. Pacifist publications such as Max Eastman's *Masses* were in danger of being banned from the mails for their criticism of the government's policies.[92] At the same time the New York *Call*'s editorial attacks upon Gompers for wanting to "Americanize" labor ("It Can't Be Done Sam"), and its insulting references to Gompers as a renegade Jew, had only degraded the publication.[93]

89. P.C.A., undated memorandum, Swarthmore.

90. Lochner to Jordan, Aug. 6, 1917, Jordan papers. No mention of this meeting was made on the floor of the Senate by any member of the Military Affairs Committee (*Congressional Record*, Senate, 65th Congress, first session, pp. 5861-5964). The New York *Call*, Aug. 10, 1917, declared that the pacifists met with some thirty congressmen.

91. New York *Times*, Aug. 9, 1917; *Congressional Record*, Senate, 65th Congress, first session, Aug. 11, 1917, pp. 5956-5957. La Follette rose and declared, "Mr. President I present a concurrent resolution which I ask to have read." Earlier, La Follette had urged the Council pacifists to get busy and elect anti-war candidates to Congress if they wanted to stop the war (New York *Call*, Aug. 1, 1917).

92. New York *Call*, Aug. 2, 1917. Postmaster General Burleson believed it essential for the well-being of the country for all "radical" journals to be suppressed. See Johnson, *The Challenge to American Freedom*, pp. 61-62, and Bell, "Background and Development," p. 315.

93. New York *Call*, July 31, 1917.

In the midst of these attacks, Gompers had continued to work for labor loyalty. He ordered Maisel to arrange a meeting of the Alliance's directors with some of New York's leading businessmen. This Beethoven Hall meeting had resulted in promises from labor and management leaders in the New York area to co-operate in keeping down dissension in the local war plants.[94] The Alliance's support of the Administration during these weeks had been in sharp contrast to the Council's stern opposition to Wilson's war policies.

Chapter 4. Labor Pacifism or Loyalty: The Search for a National Consensus

In July the Peoples Council had been branded a "pro-German" socialist organization by the conservative press of the New York area. This fact should have been enough to discourage the Council leadership from taking seriously their plans to infiltrate the skilled unions. Despite this "obstructionist" image, the Council went ahead with its plans to hold a series of anti-war rallies throughout the country. Council officials had expected initial failures until the country's laboring classes could be persuaded to adopt the national workingmen's council idea. Only then, the radicals reasoned, could the real strength of pacifism in the United States be determined. Neither their poor public image nor the A.F. of L.'s Alliance discouraged them from continuing plans to hold their national convention.[1] Such a convention, they believed, would serve to tie together the larger councils of New York, Philadelphia, San Francisco, Chicago, and Los Angeles, as well as unite the smaller councils springing up throughout the Midwest. A convention would launch the Council program to obstruct the war effort through nationwide strikes, opposition to conscription, and infiltration of the conservative labor movement. The country could

94. New York *Times*, Aug. 14, 1917; minutes, Beethoven Hall, Aug. 13, 1917, Gompers papers.

1. Organizing Committee report, P.C.A., June 28, 1917, Swarthmore. Minneapolis was the site most favored for the national convention at this time.

be covered by a network of anti-war organizations capable of dispatching orders from the New York headquarters. At this natal stage, the radicals did not give undue consideration to their initial failures.[2] Council leaders were aware that they were advocating an unpopular cause, but they hoped that as the war dragged on and the losses of the belligerents mounted, the American public would swing against the conflict. In the meantime, the leadership prepared to spread its anti-war propaganda and educate the public to the benefits of peace and a "social democracy."

Council pacifists opened their national propaganda campaign by appealing to the dissident elements in the labor movement to overthrow the old conservative order represented by the A.F. of L. and especially by Gompers who was "sitting upon the Council for National Defense with John D. Rockefeller . . . who never wooed the workingmen until crisis threatened"[3]—a leader who had proved "indifferent to the labor movement."[4] Anti-war laborers were urged to join a campaign to "wage war against war" by flooding their newspapers with letters calling for immediate peace until "the voice of the radical is heard."[5] Similarly, the leadership distributed John D. Works's pamphlet, "Why We Are At War," which accused Wilson of being a "weak vacillating man" who had allied America with the most imperialistic nations in the world.[6]

Meanwhile, Council speakers played upon the sympathies of those like the fiery intellectual Randolph Bourne, who believed "It must never be forgotten that in each community it was the least liberal and the least democratic elements among whom the preparedness and late war sentiment was found." A month later Bourne expressed the views of many anti-war radicals more forthrightly when he wrote, "The initiative for peace has passed from

2. The pacifists took in stride their chances of being jailed or imprisoned for spreading sedition. The council movement had even spread into the Army where a pacifist soldier was caught distributing Council propaganda. He was charged with violating Section III of the Espionage Act and placed under $5,000 bond (Victor J. McCone to Robert McKnight, Sept. 3, 1917, Socialist Party papers, Correspondence 1916-1918, Duke University).

3. "Call for a National Convention," P.C.A. publication, July, 1917, Swarthmore.

4. "Workingmens Council of America," P.C.A. publication, *ibid.*

5. "Dear Fighting Pacifist," P.C.A. circular, *ibid.*

6. John D. Works, "Why We Are At War," *ibid.*

President Wilson into the hands of the Council for Workingmen and Soldiers deputies."[7]

Against this background, Council pacifists contacted every major peace society in the country and appealed for them to send delegates to Minneapolis. Again the Council's extreme image hampered its effectiveness, and a response from the other societies was not always obtained easily. A case in point was the difficulty with which the American Union Against Militarism reached its decision to co-operate in the national convention.

There were large numbers of Council members in the A.U.A.M. who were interested in melding that organization into the movement as had been done with the Emergency Peace Federation. Because of this situation many peace societies hesitated to give their support to the Council for fear of losing their independence. Nevertheless, the struggle over A.U.A.M. autonomy got under way when Paul Kellogg, a member of both organizations, suggested that the A.U.A.M. co-operate with the Council at Minneapolis. Lillian Wald, who earlier in May had objected to the workingmen's council idea, rose to block the motion. Miss Wald objected to her organization becoming a part of a movement which had already been branded as extremist.[8] She felt so strongly about this fact that she threatened to resign from the A.U.A.M. if it cooperated with the Council convention.[9] The A.U.A.M. Executive Committee, however, contained enough Council members to ensure the organization's co-operation, and the committee voted to send Roger Baldwin and Norman Thomas to Minneapolis. Outnumbered, Miss Wald reluctantly agreed with this decision but insisted that the A.U.A.M. should decide once and for all whether it wished to be absorbed by the Council or remain an autonomous organization.[10] The struggle over the A.U.A.M. autonomy issue

7. R. S. Bourne, "The Seven Arts," "The War and the Intellectuals," and "The Collapse of the American Strategy," as cited in Carl Resek, ed., *War and the Intellectuals: Collected Essays, 1915-1919* (New York, 1964).

8. A.U.A.M. minutes, Aug. 6, 1917, Swarthmore; Ward to Crystal Eastman, Aug. 28, 1917, copy, Jordan papers.

9. Wald to A.U.A.M., Aug. 27, 1917, A.U.A.M. papers, Swarthmore.

10. A.U.A.M. minutes, Aug. 30, 1917, *ibid*. The A.U.A.M. broke apart over the question of supporting the Council. Frank Walsh resigned because his support went to the Wilson Administration, while Paul Kellogg and Scott Nearing resigned because the A.U.A.M. would not join the council movement (A.U.A.M. minutes, Sept. 13, 1917, *ibid*.).

showed to what lengths Council pacifists would go to procreate their movement. It was clear that they owed their loyalty to an idea and not to any particular agency.

By August 13, elaborate Council plans had been completed to transport the delegates to and from Minneapolis. Advantage was to be taken of the long routes from the East and West coasts: special trains to carry the delegations also would provide opportunities for spontaneous peace rallies to be held along the way.[11] One special train, scheduled to leave New York City on August 30, was to be equipped with an observation car, a parlor car, and a library car.[12] Council officials were requested to ride the trains and lead a peace rally at each stop. As Lella Secor put it, "The special trains offer the opportunity for much propaganda which must not be overlooked."[13] Stops were planned at Albany, Utica, Syracuse, Rochester, Erie, Toledo, and Chicago, where the largest delegation was expected to board. Jacob Panken announced that more than two thousand delegates would arrive in Minneapolis aboard these two trains.[14] Council officials hoped that this method of transportation would provide a master stroke of propaganda for their cause.[15]

But the Minneapolis convention soon faced difficulties. The local press, upon learning that their city had been chosen for the Council's convention, unleashed a bitter attack against the pacifists for being "pro-German" as well as extreme in endorsing the Bolshevik peace proposals. The newspapers of the area combined with the loyalty leagues of Minnesota in stirring up public opinion against the convention. As this adverse publicity made the headlines elsewhere in the country, Council officials found it increasingly difficult to sign up delegates. When Gompers suddenly expressed interest in holding a rival Alliance convention in the same place, the newspapers rapidly played up the entire episode as a struggle between right and wrong.[16]

11. Organizing Committee report, P.C.A., June 28, 1917, Swarthmore.
12. Bishop Paul Jones to Jordan, Aug. 13, 1917, Jordan papers.
13. Lella Secor, memorandum, Aug. 27, 1917, P.C.A. file, Swarthmore.
14. New York *Call*, Aug. 17, 1917.
15. P.C.A. *Bulletin*, Vol. I, No. 2, Aug. 16, 1917, Swarthmore; also Lochner to Jordan, Aug. 22, 1917, Jordan papers.
16. Organizing Committee report, P.C.A., Aug. 19, 1917, Swarthmore. Gompers at this time had succeeded in stirring up feelings against Max Pine and the United Hebrew Trades for co-operating with the Council

Meanwhile, events in Minneapolis went from bad to worse. Lochner, who had traveled there to secure a convention site, discovered to his dismay that all the halls and auditoriums were suddenly closed against him,[17] largely because the powerful Minnesota State Federation of Labor had condemned the Council and proclaimed its loyalty to the Alliance.[18] Finding himself unable to rent a hall, Lochner took the drastic step of securing a large convention tent, but he discovered that no one would rent him the land on which to erect the tent.[19] Yet these problems only hardened the pacifists' determination to hold their convention. As James Maurer expressed it, "I had some reservations as to the Minneapolis meeting, but now that I know Spargo-Gompers and Company are going I am for being there."[20]

Council officials struck back at those causing their problems in Minneapolis. The New York *Call* blamed the loyalist Public Safety Committee of Minnesota as well as the political enemies of Mayor Thomas Van Lear for the Council's troubles.[21] Van Lear, a socialist and a member of the Council, had not only publicly promised the Council a safe meeting in Minneapolis but had promised to address the convention.[22] The "business press" of Minnesota also was accused of creating trouble,[23] or as Rebecca Shelly put it, "Those forces which during the past three months have been harrying us. . . ."[24] Lochner referred to all the troublemakers as "Guardians of Supernationalism,"[25] which was an indirect slam at the Alliance. Gompers, however, simply wrote that it had been the "city fathers" of Minneapolis who aroused public opinion against the Council convention.[26] It is certain that the Alliance was not behind the opposition to the Council in Minneapolis. Far

(New York *Call*, Aug. 14, 1917); Pine, in turn, accused Gompers of being "in league with Wall Street" in supporting the Wilson Administration (*ibid.*, Aug. 19, 1917).

17. New York *Times*, Aug. 22, 1917.
18. *Ibid.*, Aug. 23, 1917.
19. Lochner, *Always the Unexpected*, pp. 68-69.
20. New York *Call*, Aug. 22, 1917.
21. *Ibid.*
22. *Ibid.*, Aug. 24, 1917.
23. Organizing Committee for the Minnesota Convention, minutes, P.C.A., Aug. 19, 1917, Swarthmore.
24. P.C.A. circular, Aug. 28, 1917, *ibid.*
25. Lochner, *Always the Unexpected*, p. 68.
26. Gompers, *Seventy Years*, II, 382.

from wanting the pacifists driven out of the city, the Alliance preferred to reap the propaganda value of a rival convention.[27]

Despite their serious problems in Minneapolis, Council officials went ahead and issued a call for their convention: "Shall we stand with the high sounding American Alliance for Labor and Democracy and Gompers, or the Peoples Council for Labor and Democracy of James Maurer. . . . Samuel Gompers despite his noble duty of the earlier days no longer speaks for American labor. . . . Come to Minneapolis!"[28] With unswerving determination the pacifists released an immediate national appeal for $5,000 to finance the convention[29] and an additional $50,000 for future needs.[30] Their only course of action was to forge ahead with their plans or admit that there was not enough public support for the peace movement to launch a national organization.[31]

While this contention was raging, Lochner was doing his best to find a convention site for the pacifists. He had welcomed Van Lear's promise to protect the Council in Minneapolis; but Governor J. A. Burnquist, angered that a radical convention was to be held in his state, declared the Council to be unwelcome in Minnesota.[32] Realizing that a convention in Minneapolis was now out of the question, Lochner traveled to Hudson, Wisconsin, where there was suppose to be a large contingent of socialists. But, again as in Minneapolis, Hudson's city fathers, fearing disorder if the pacifists gathered in their town, met Lochner with a lynching rope and a waiting train. Lochner hastily left town.[33] From Hudson

27. Maisel to Gompers, Aug. 20, 1917, Gompers papers. By this date plans were ready to hold the Alliance convention in Minneapolis. Charges that the Alliance prevented the Council from meeting in Minneapolis do not appear correct. See David Shanon, *The Socialist Party of America: A History* (New York, 1955), p. 117. The New York *Call*, Aug. 30, 1917, printed Gompers' regrets that the Alliance would not face the Council in Minneapolis.

28. P.C.A. *Bulletin*, Vol. I, No. 3, Aug. 27, 1917, Swarthmore.

29. P.C.A. press release, undated, New York Public Library.

30. P.C.A. press release, undated, Swarthmore.

31. Norman Thomas to Wald, Aug. 27, 1917, Thomas papers, Box 3. Thomas wrote: "The council movement must not fail at Minneapolis or we will have to use whatever organization is now possible for pacifist thought . . ." (New York *Call*, Aug. 29, 1917). The *Call* blamed "money interests and war profiteers" for the Council's troubles.

32. Lochner to James W. Fawcett, telegram, undated copy, Swarthmore.

33. Lochner, *Always the Unexpected*, pp. 68-70; New York *Times*, Sept. 2, 1917; New York *Call*, Aug. 31, 1917.

he traveled to Fargo, North Dakota, where Governor Frazier had indicated earlier that he might allow the Council to meet.[34] Again, the citizens of Fargo's loyalty societies whipped up resentment against the idea, and Lochner thought it better to move on.[35] The New York *Times* gleefully published these embarrassing incidents and teased: "The pacifists cannot find a place to hold their meeting. They wander in the Midwest as homeless men."[36]

As this comic opera plot unfolded, Mayor William Hale Thompson extended an invitation for the Council to meet under his personal protection in Chicago.[37] Lochner jumped at the opportunity, not only because time was precious, but because he was running out of convention sites. A tentative date of September 1 had been set for the convention and the delegates were preparing to board their trains. Again misfortune struck. Governor Frank Lowden of Illinois, learning of Mayor Thompson's offer, immediately telephoned Thompson not to allow the pacifists to meet in Chicago. The Mayor, however, stood his ground and insisted that the Council members had a constitutional right to assemble where they wished. As the *Times* remarked, "there was complete confusion."[38] The Chicago press, learning of the disagreement between the Mayor and the Governor, played upon the political as well as the loyalty questions involved. All in all, it was a reporter's holiday.[39] For the pacifists this was the last straw, and in desperation they hurriedly sent a telegram to President Wilson calling his attention to their harassment and asserting their constitutional right to free assembly.[40] At the moment the telegram reached the White House, Wilson was preparing a letter to Samuel Gompers on several matters to "guarantee democracy at home."[41]

34. New York *Call*, Aug. 30, 1917.

35. New York *Times*, Aug. 30, 1917; New York *Call*, Sept. 5, 1917.

36. New York *Times*, Sept. 1, 1917.

37. Lochner, *Always the Unexpected*, p. 70; New York *Call*, Sept. 1, 1917.

38. William T. Hutchinson, *Lowden of Illinois* (Chicago, 1957), I, 378-380; New York *Times*, Sept. 1, 1917.

39. John J. Symes to Attorney General of the United States, Jan. 11, 1919, Record Group 60, Justice Department files, National Archives. Included here is a Justice Department investigation of the Lowden-Thompson dispute, which casts doubts on Thompson's loyalty.

40. Organizational report for the National Convention of the P.C.A., Aug. 31, 1917, Swarthmore.

41. Baker, *Woodrow Wilson: Life and Letters*, VII, 247-248.

There is no indication that the President heeded the telegram. Events soon got out of hand in Chicago. While Thompson and Lowden squabbled over the convention, approximately two hundred pacifists arrived in the city on August 31, almost half of them from the West Coast. The Dearborn Hotel, which became the pacifists' headquarters, was surrounded immediately by local police meant for their protection. The delegates rented a nearby auditorium and the first session quickly got under way on the morning of September 1.[42] The radicals worked with the haste of those who knew that they were sitting on a powder keg. They quickly approved a constitution calling on all anti-war radicals to support the Bolshevik peace proposals and build a "social democracy" similar to that of socialist Russia.[43] That afternoon the delegates reassembled to set up a national administrative council consisting of a general committee of fifty, an executive committee of fifteen, and numerous subcommittees based on national districts.[44]

It was not long before Governor Lowden learned that the pacifists were meeting in Chicago, and he hurriedly telephoned Mayor Thompson to halt the proceedings. But the Mayor was out of town, and in his absence Police Chief Herman Schuetler received the order. Schuetler hastily collected a riot squad and drove to the auditorium where he and his men burst into the building and rushed to the stage where lawyer Seymour Stedman was speaking. Pushing him aside the officers cleared the stage and ordered the convention closed. When Stedman refused to leave, he was arrested and physically forced from the building. During this confusion Rebecca Shelly leaped to her feet and demanded to be arrested also, but the officers hesitated to arrest a woman and simply carried her from the building. The remaining delegates were herded together and pushed outside, after which the doors were closed and locked. Under the threat of arrest if they returned, the delegates slowly filed back to the Dearborn Hotel and completed their work in their own rooms. That afternoon, Morris Hillquit was elected national chairman of the Council and Lochner retained the directorship. The other officers remained the same,

42. New York *Call*, Sept. 1, 1917.
43. P.C.A. *Constitution*, Chicago, Sept. 1, 1917, copy, Swarthmore.
44. P.C.A. *Bulletin*, Vol. I, No. 4, Sept. 1-2, 1917, Tamiment Institute.

including that of treasurer, which in Jordan's absence was not taken from him as he had requested. For this reason, Jordan finally dissociated himself from the movement once and for all.[45]

The next morning in defiance of the Governor and Chief Schuetler, the delegates returned to the auditorium, unlocked the doors, and moved inside. Shortly thereafter, Mayor Thompson returned to town and ordered his Chief of Police to allow the pacifists to continue their convention.[46] But the delegates were uneasy that Governor Lowden might again overrule Thompson's order to his police and jail the entire delegation. While the convention proceeded, H. H. Merrick of the Chicago Security League, learning that the delegates had reassembled, hurriedly telephoned Springfield and informed Lowden of the news. Outraged that Thompson had disobeyed his orders, Lowden mobilized three companies of National Guard troops and ordered them to Chicago to close the convention.[47]

While the troops were on their way, the delegates proceeded with their business. Rabbi Judah Magnes delivered another hard-hitting speech attacking Wilson's stand for total victory. He asserted that the President failed to realize that the German people, who were not responsible for the war, would suffer the most from this policy.[48] Magnes was followed by Senator William E. Mason, who made a dramatic appeal for freedom of speech, and former Senator John Works, who asked the harassed delegates if American democracy were no better than German autocracy. In response several Russian-born delegates cried out that the police action of the previous day was as bad as anything they had seen in Tsarist Russia.[49]

At this point Seymour Stedman, who had been released on bail, received word that the National Guard was on its way to the auditorium. Dramatically leaping onto the stage, Stedman suggested

45. P.C.A. Chicago convention, minutes, Sept. 1, 1917, Swarthmore; New York *Times*, Sept. 2, 1917; New York *Call*, Sept. 2, 1917. The *Call* stated that some 250 delegates were forced from the auditorium in a "prussian-like raid."
46. P.C.A. Chicago convention, minutes, Sept. 2, 1917, Swarthmore.
47. Hutchinson, *Lowden of Illinois*, I, 378-379.
48. Rabbi Judah L. Magnes, address, Chicago, Sept. 2, 1917, copy, Tamiment Institute.
49. New York *Call*, Sept. 3, 1917; William E. Mason, speech, Chicago, Sept. 2, 1917, Swarthmore.

that the delegates adjourn to the hotel before the Guard could arrive; but they refused to budge. At 7 P.M. when the day's work was completed, there had still been no sign of the Guard. At 8 P.M., however, the troops pulled up in front of the auditorium and rushed inside. The commander discovered much to his embarrassment that the pacifists had already adjourned and that the auditorium had been taken over by a wedding party.[50]

The next morning the Council delegates boarded their trains and headed home. The convention had only increased their notoriety because the country's loyal press had billed the gathering as "pro-German." The episode had been humiliating to the pacifists, and especially so to Lochner who had borne the brunt of the insults. Yet there was a bright side to their situation. The Chicago incident had given them an excellent opportunity to assume the role of martyrs suffering for the freedoms of speech and assembly at home while the Wilson Administration professed to be fighting a crusade for democracy abroad. But the pacifists were not deprived of their own supporters, many of whom believed as Jane Addams did that the entire episode had been distorted by the press.[51] The New York *Call*, as the loyal organ of the Socialist party, gave the Council its full sympathy by proclaiming that the organization only asked for the traditional American freedoms of speech and assembly.[52]

While the pacifists were undergoing their tribulations in the Midwest, Alliance officials were busily preparing for their own loyalty convention in Minneapolis. Despite their disappointment at not being able to appear in the same city with the pacifists, the officials worked hard to launch a national movement. The primary job of working out this program fell upon the shoulders of Robert Maisel, who asked Chairman Gompers to keynote the Minneapolis meeting. Gompers readily agreed.[53] Maisel then asked Charles E. Russell and James Duncan of the recently returned

50. Lochner, *Always the Unexpected*, p. 71; New York *Times*, Sept. 3, 1917.

51. Addams, *Peace and Bread*, p. 144. New York *Call*, Sept. 4, 1917, declared that the Chicago police protected the Council's delegates from the Guard.

52. New York *Call*, Sept. 4, 1917.

53. Maisel to Gompers, telegram, Aug. 20, 1917, Gompers papers.

Root mission from Russia to appear and speak of their experiences. The purpose of Maisel's request was clear: The presence of the mission would demonstrate the close bond between Wilson, the A.F. of L., and the pro-war radicals.[54]

As for the remaining pro-war socialists, Spargo was still working out plans to create a new socialist movement. He badly wanted his faction represented at Minneapolis with the A.F. of L. delegates: "I realize that our old friend Gompers has gotten to the point where he needs us and is therefore trying to use us, on the other hand, we need the A.F. of L."[55] The next day he wrote Creel, who was helping Maisel plan the convention: "It has been running through my mind that some special effort must be made to take the wind entirely out of the sails of the so-called Peoples Council . . . pro-war socialists must speak at Minneapolis."[56] If Creel were aware of Spargo's desire to create a dual movement, he did not indicate so, for on August 29 he asked Spargo to write America's war objectives into pamphlet form.[57] Nor did he object when J. G. Phelps Stokes agreed to serve as treasurer of the national Alliance, "provided Gompers and the others protect me financially."[58]

Creel and Maisel continued with their organization of the convention. Maisel planned to transport the Alliance delegates to Minneapolis in the same manner used by the pacifists. But this time "red, white and blue" specials were to leave each coast and pick up delegates along the way.[59] On August 25 Maisel explained these plans to Gompers, who promised the complete co-operation of his office.[60] But the Alliance needed a maximum propaganda effort at Minneapolis, and with this in mind Gompers asked President Wilson to address the delegates. Wilson, however, was far too busy to attend. He sent instead an official endorsement which made it perfectly clear where his sympathy lay: "We must organize at home. . . . I have read with pride of those who are to take

54. New York *Times*, Aug. 19, 1917.
55. Spargo to R. D. Sawyer, Aug 23, 1917, Stokes papers, Box 27.
56. Spargo to Creel, Aug. 24, 1917, C.P.I. papers, 1-A1-39.
57. Creel to Spargo, Aug. 29, 1917, Spargo papers.
58. Stokes to Maisel, Aug. 22, 1917, Stokes papers, Box 27.
59. Maisel to Gompers, Aug. 23, 1917, Gompers papers.
60. Maisel to Gompers, Aug. 25, 1917; Gompers to Maisel, Aug. 26, 1917, *ibid.*

part in Minneapolis. We need to educate the radical groups."[61]
With the President's official endorsement in his pocket, Gompers
urged all A.F. of L. unions to send delegates to Minneapolis so
"that bona fide labor might be safeguarded and the rights of the
workers protected."[62]

Few labor delegations have left New York City with as good
publicity as the Alliance members received. Grand Central Station
was draped with red, white, and blue pennants, as well as the
flags of the Allied nations. Military bands stirred the crowd with
patriotic marches, and Louise Homer, one of America's great ope-
ratic contraltos, sang the "Star-Spangled Banner," while an honor
guard of French, Italian, and British soldiers stood at attention
beside the tracks.[63] With the cheers of the crowd still ringing in
their ears, the delegates boarded the train and turned toward
Minneapolis feeling themselves to be very much a part of Wilson's
crusade for democracy.

Minneapolis welcomed the Alliance delegations with open
arms on September 4. The city's papers, which had earlier been
so hostile toward the Council, were loud in their praise of labor's
loyal stand behind the war effort. Members of the Minnesota
Federation of Labor who had boycotted the Council's convention
mingled with the Alliance delegates and even provided them with
free transportation between the hotels and the convention site.
At the same time the city fathers gave several luncheons for the
Alliance. The welcome had been organized by the local loyalty
leagues, which even provided a band for the enjoyment of those
Alliance officials staying in the Andrews Hotel.[64]

The convention opened the next morning and the delegates
spent the day setting up committees. That night Gompers keynoted the session with an address in which he explained that the

61. Wilson to Gompers, Aug. 27, 1917, Wilson papers. Gompers had
warned the Council of National Defense on August 25 that if justice were
not done to labor at home during the war he could not hold the line
against the pacifists and socialists (Cronon, ed., *Cabinet Diaries of Josephus
Daniels*, p. 196).

62. Circular from Gompers to all locals, Aug. 29, 1917, Gompers
papers.

63. New York *Times*, Sept. 2, 1917.

64. *Ibid.*, Sept. 5, 1917. The "Gompers Circus," a press copy article,
unsigned, written for publication in the Socialist Party of America Labor
magazine, copy, Socialist Party papers, File 1910-1930, Duke University.

Alliance was "to bring together the A.F. of L. and pro-war socialists into a working organization for the immediate purpose of winning the war." Gompers promised that the A.F. of L. intended to co-operate fully with the Wilson Administration until Germany was decisively defeated. The government urged all Americans, Gompers declared, to join with the Alliance in keeping the country united behind the war effort. To illustrate dramatically the Administration's support of the Alliance, Gompers took Wilson's message from his pocket and read it to the delegates.[65] It was clear that the President endorsed the A.F. of L.'s over-all loyalty program.

In response to the President's plea for unity, the pro-war socialist delegation made a profession of faith to the Administration. Spargo led the group by bitterly attacking his former socialist friends for deserting the war effort and becoming "tools of Germany."[66] His speech was the signal for the others to declare their loyalty. Charles E. Russell made perhaps the most dramatic declaration of them all when, in reference to Senator Robert M. La Follette, he cried, "I admit that I have been a friend of Robert La Follette in the past, but in this supreme hour I have no brother, I have nothing but the Republic!"[67] Unity was apparent when Governor Burnquist, who had earlier driven the Council from Minneapolis, showed up with a bodyguard of troops to welcome the convention. But the meeting was strictly for loyalists; when a reporter from the New York *Call* tried to enter the auditorium, he was hastily turned away.[68]

On the third and last day of the convention there was another display of unity between the A.F. of L. delegates and the pro-war socialists, who had held several separate conferences to co-ordi-

65. New York *Times*, Sept. 6, 1917; Gompers, speech, Minneapolis, Sept. 6, 1917, Gompers papers; Wilson to Gompers, telegram, copy, C.P.I. papers, 1-A1-26. The New York *Call*, Sept. 7, 1917, claimed that Gompers was received coldly at Minneapolis by a small delegation of 125 men of "the Gompers' stripe." The lack of participation from the A.F. of L.'s unions at Minneapolis is probably attributable to the quickness with which the convention was assembled and not to any disagreement over Gompers' stand in regard to the Wilson Administration.

66. New York *Times*, Sept. 6, 1917. The New York *Call*, Sept. 7, 1917, reported that Spargo had sold out to the Alliance.

67. New York *Times*, Sept. 7, 1917; *Proceedings*, A.F. of L., 1917, pp. 97-98.

68. New York *Call*, Sept. 7, 8, 1917.

nate their support of the Alliance. But this unity was deceptive. Spargo had shrewdly used the convention to further his own plans to organize a new socialist movement; or as Stokes put it, "We took advantage of all the socialists there to exchange our views."[69] Nevertheless, Stokes loyally accepted the position of treasurer, and Spargo did not hesitate to keep the first vice-presidency, a position second only to that held by Gompers.[70] The convention ended in an apparent display of good will with a speech by Clarence Darrow, who had dropped in to show his support for the movement, and with the new officers holding hands while the audience applauded this dramatic rapprochment between the A.F. of L. and the pro-war socialists.

Despite the low attendance, which was the result of Gompers' determination to assemble hurriedly in Minneapolis,[71] the Alliance convention had appeared to be a complete success. As a result, the Alliance, Gompers, and the A.F. of L. emerged from Minneapolis as the champions of "Americanism," the leaders of the popular cause. Gompers added to this image in Chicago where he declared his intentions not to use the "Americanization" of labor to attain any political goals.[72] By September, 1917, the Alliance had started its campaign to swing the majority of the A.F. of L.'s unions behind the Wilson Administration's war program.

The convention was hardly over when the Alliance came in for some high praise from the floor of Congress. Senator Chamberlain of Oregon, probably remembering his earlier encounter with the Peoples Council delegation, rose to exclaim, "Every word and every line of their [Alliance] resolutions breathe the spirit of splendid patriotism. . . . How different the so-called Peoples Council of America's traitorous and seditious expressions. . . ."[73] The New York *Times*, which had given the Alliance prime coverage, asserted that the organization was now prepared to "smoke out

69. Stokes to W. E. Walling, Sept. 7, 1917, Stokes papers, Box 28.
70. Spargo, circular to pro-war socialist friends, Sept. 13, 1917, *ibid.*
71. Organizational Committee for the American Alliance for Labor and Democracy, minutes, Minneapolis, Sept. 7, 1917, Gompers papers; Chicago *Daily News*, Sept. 8, 1917; Frank Morris to Stokes, Sept. 11, 1917, Stokes papers, Box 28. Morris claimed that the Alliance collected only some $300 at Minneapolis.
72. Gompers, speech, Sept. 14, 1917, Gompers papers.
73. *Congressional Record*, Senate, 65th Congress, first session, Sept. 7, 1917, 6737-6738.

the German agitators in the United States," "to offer its hand to all pro-war radicals," and "to unite all patriotic socialists who were interested in aiding their country like all other loyal Americans."[74] Paul Kellogg, editor of *Survey*, however, could only write, "Socialists and Unionists Hang Together."[75]

By the end of September the Alliance had started its national program to "Americanize" the radical unions. Gompers was confident that the Alliance would be a major step in building a respectable labor movement which would convince both the government and the public that the A.F. of L. could be trusted to share national responsibilities. For the Council, however, its national convention had been somewhat less than a success. Yet, like the idealists they were, Council officials believed they could convince the American public that world peace and a "social democracy" could be brought about only if workingmen crossed over to socialism.

Chapter 5. The National Programs

After the completion of the national conventions, the Alliance and the Council began spreading their respective brands of propaganda throughout the country. The Council had begun organizing on the grass-roots level much earlier than the Alliance and therefore had gained a head start over the pro-war agency. The radicals immediately called upon the country's anti-war forces to join with "the radical, the progressive, the socialist, and the agrarian," and "despite the forces of reactionism" to work for a social democracy similar to that being built by the Russian socialists. At the same time, the Council promised to take an active part in the international peace movement by maintaining contacts with similar peace societies in England and France. In this, they proclaimed their support for the international socialist movement.[1]

The Council's own program differed from that of the Ameri-

74. New York *Times*, Sept. 8-11, 13, 1917.
75. Paul Kellogg, "Socialists and Unionists Hang Together," *Survey* (Sept. 22, 1917), p. 558.

1. Scott Nearing, "The Peoples Council of America," P.C.A. publication, copy, Tamiment Institute.

can Socialist party by its emphasis on a society consisting of local workers' soviets in each industry. Thus the Council was a bit further to the left than the majority of American socialists of that day. Yet radicals like James Maurer, Max Pine, and Morris Hillquit worked for the council movement while holding responsible positions in the Socialist party.[2] The fact that these socialists worked for a more extreme organization meant little, since the party sought to use the Council as an ally against the Wilson Administration. Socialists like Hillquit had no intention of allowing their party to be taken over by the pro-soviet Council. The party would lose little by supporting the Council's programs, while at the same time it would gain the support of an additional pacifist element against the war effort.

Whether it was the pacifists or the socialists who worked for a "social democracy," their programs came into direct conflict with those of the A.F. of L., for the Federation's policy of cooperating with capitalism had produced, according to both groups of radicals, "the minimum labor standards." What they offered the American worker was a chance to overthrow capitalism, to instal a social control of prices and wages, and to obtain a greater share of the national wealth. This would never be accomplished under Gompers' direction, they stressed, and only a turn to the left by conservative labor would ever bring about a real democracy for the working classes.[3] Both organizations emphasized that the war was not a workers' war. They urged the non-socialist unions to take a stand against capitalism by overturning their present "reactionary" government for one built on solid socialist principles.[4]

Whether or not the non-socialist unions would support the pacifists and socialists was in question in the fall of 1917, for there was no indication that the average worker was about to turn against capitalism. The facts indicated otherwise. But the real danger of the pacifist-socialist alliance was in its threat to draw those who were unhappy with capitalism into one obstructionist movement. If the war went poorly for the Allies, and if

2. "Council to Protect Labor's Standards During the War," P.C.A. publication, copy, Swarthmore.
3. "Peoples Council on Industrial Standards," *ibid.*
4. "The Truth About the Peoples Council," *ibid.*

labor's standards dropped badly at home, all the dissenting elements within labor might well rally to the pacifist-socialist cause. This possibility had worried Gompers and Wilson and had caused the creation of the Alliance to check left-wing agitation in labor before it could disrupt the war program.[5]

Among the groups whom Wilson and Gompers feared might be sympathetic to the council movement were thousands of Jews employed in the garment industry of the East. Many of these people had fled the persecutions of tsarist Russia and were not unhappy now that the Tsar had been overthrown by the socialists. Many other Jews had migrated from Germany, France, and Italy as converts to socialism. In America thousands of them had settled in New York's garment industry where they worked under terrible sweatshop conditions. These people supported the liberal United Hebrew Trades, the *Forward*, and the Amalgamated Clothing Workers of America, all of whose officials were in the Council. Consequently, the garment industry proved a prime recruiting target for Council organizers, who hoped to organize all those Jews supporting socialist Russia and socialism in general.[6]

The Alliance first concentrated on keeping New York's East Side Jews loyal to the Administration by employing Jewish organizers, like Jacob Chykin, to work in that area. After looking the situation over, Chykin suggested that the Alliance move in quickly with an effective loyalty program before the Council's organizers (directed from the offices of the *Forward*) could take over the district.[7] The Alliance acted quickly and immediately broadcast its intentions to "loyalize" the East Side.[8]

Most of America's second and third generation Jews were more politically moderate than their newly arrived brethren. Many older Jews were solid businessmen and capitalists who stood to lose much if the Council's social program was adopted. Although they had not been enthusiastic over the government of tsarist Russia, they were not in favor of the Bolsheviks either. Rabbi Stephen

5. William Z. Foster, *Misleaders of Labor* (New York, 1927), pp. 54-55; Nathan Fine, *Labor and Farmers' Parties in the United States, 1828-1928* (New York, 1928), p. 219.

6. Rowland H. Harvey, *Samuel Gompers: Champion Of the Toiling Masses* (Stanford, 1935), pp. 219-220

7. Jacob Chykin, report, Sept. 10, 1917, Gompers papers.

8. New York *Times*, Sept. 16, 1917.

S. Wise, the Alliance's counterpart of the Council's Rabbi Judah L. Magnes, emerged as the leader of these Jews who formed the Jewish Socialist League to support the war effort.[9] The League's close co-operation with the government gave the Alliance a chance to organize most of these East Side Jews into the loyalist movement. The New York *Times* played no slight part in this effort by repeatedly condemning any Jew who proved "disloyal" to his country.[10]

The Alliance's officials were aware that the success of their program depended on gaining the loyalty of the Jewish worker; or as Chester Wright put it, "The Alliance will have trouble organizing . . . if it is simply a flag waving organization without sympathy for the labor movement."[11] Alliance organizers worked diligently among the Jewish laborers to convince them that their best interests lay with American capitalism which was more democratic than the capitalism of Western Europe.[12] To point out that labor pacifism was the same as disloyalty, the Alliance distributed on the East Side a pamphlet, "The Disloyal Pacifists," which accused the leaders of the Council-socialist alliance—Nearing, Hillquit, Berger, and Debs—of being "un-American" because they opposed the war program of their own government.[13] To stress further the workers' importance to the war effort, Chester Wright wrote a series of pamphlets emphasizing America's need for "loyal" laborers who would be "a factor in the shaping of world destinies!"[14] The inference to Wilsonian idealism was undeniable.

The effort to "Americanize" labor concentrated not only on the Jewish worker but on any segment of labor which did not support the war effort. In Rhode Island the Alliance organizer, Herman Robinson, worked among Providence's non-Jewish immigrant groups and succeeded in setting up a local chapter which pledged to "faithfully and loyally support the war for justice, freedom and democracy to a triumphant conclusion. . . ."[15] In the Midwest Clarence Darrow diligently worked among those German-

9. *Ibid.*, Sept. 14, 1917.
10. *Ibid.*, Sept. 18, 1917.
11. Chester Wright to Gompers, Sept. 21, 1917, Gompers papers.
12. "Why We Are at War," American Alliance publication, copy, *ibid.*
13. "The Disloyal Pacifist," *ibid.*
14. Chester Wright, "Bugle Calls for Labor," *ibid.*
15. Herman Robinson to Gompers, Sept. 19, 1917, *ibid.*

Americans who dreaded seeing their Fatherland humiliated by the total defeat policy called for by Wilson.[16] Darrow, who in 1914 had supported the anti-war cause, now recovered from his earlier pacifist leanings "in the twinkling of an eye."[17] Although he was keenly aware of the strong pro-German sympathy in certain areas of the Midwest, he never fully accepted the techniques necessary to run an effective loyalist agency like the Alliance. He was continually critical of any propaganda which tended to stir up national hatred against a particular pacifist group. This attitude made his relationship with the Alliance a strained one.[18]

Working with Darrow in the Midwest was the pro-war socialist W. R. Gaylord of Wisconsin. Gaylord proved invaluable to the Alliance in organizing those socialists who were lukewarm toward the war.[19] He alone helped to found some twenty-one Alliance chapters in that area. Despite this he was forced to admit that pro-German sympathy was so strong in Wisconsin that the state's loyalty was questionable.[20] Gaylord warned Gompers that the Alliance must not wait too long to organize this area or "Robert M. La Follette would have the entire State in the pacifist camp."[21]

The Alliance's work in the Midwest was hampered seriously by Spargo's determination to help in the organization of a new National party to be composed of prohibitionists, single-taxers, progressives, and his own pro-war faction. Spargo had been upset for some time at the treatment given the socialists in Minneapolis and now hinted that the National party would be more sympathetic to radicals of all shades.[22] Statements of this kind were obviously intended to bring "borderline" radicals into the new movement. As Gaylord organized for the Alliance, he came under

16. Alfred Jacques to Wilson, Sept. 3, 1917, Wilson papers.
17. Clarence Darrow, *The Story of My Life* (New York, 1934), p. 210.
18. Irving Stone, *Clarence Darrow for the Defense* (New York, 1941), p. 336.
19. Gaylord to Gompers, Sept. 28, 1917, Gompers papers.
20. Gaylord to Gompers, Sept. 21, 28, 1917, *ibid.* Creel was so concerned about pacifism in Utah, too, that he wrote Governor Bamberger about the situation. The Governor, who was sympathetic to the pacifists, denied the charges (Bamberger to Creel, Sept. 28, 1917, C.P.I. papers, 1-A1-1).
21. Gaylord to Gompers, Oct. 5, 1917, Gompers papers.
22. "Pacifist Pilgrims," *Literary Digest*, LV (Sept. 15, 1917), 16-17; Harry L. Laidler, *Socialism in Thought and Action* (New York, 1925), p. 459.

pressure to organize for Spargo's group also. As a loyal socialist, Gaylord hesitated to interfere with Spargo's work and closed his eyes to the dual party.

It was at this point that Gompers became aware for the first time that Spargo was putting pressure on Gaylord to work for the National party. Knowing full well that the Alliance would not survive dualism within its ranks, Gompers decided to insist that Gaylord reject Spargo's requests for assistance. He got in touch with Gaylord and threatened to cut off funds for his organizing work. Gaylord suddenly found himself caught between Spargo's demands on the one hand, his loyalty to the Alliance, and Gompers' determination to stop this dualism. He eventually yielded to Gompers, however, and pledged to support only the Alliance's program, but not until he had declared that Spargo's plans contained some merit.[23]

Gompers had no intention of allowing Spargo to form a third party, and he gave Chester Wright, whose loyalty he believed secure, the task of reaching a better understanding with the Alliance's pro-war socialists. Wright's first task was to tell Gaylord of Gompers' pledge that the Alliance would not seek to control its radical members. Wright's promise reassured Gaylord that his friends would not be "strangled" by the Alliance as Spargo had hinted. He therefore went about his organizing work in the Midwest.[24]

At the same time, Gompers had turned to Spargo as the key to putting down the disruption. As usual Gompers had learned much about Spargo's plans from the faithful Maisel. Angered at Spargo's brazen attempts to use him and the A.F. of L. to advance a dual socialist movement, Gompers declared, "I cannot understand what purpose can be accomplished by this. I promised to give them all cooperation in the Alliance and now they form a new party."[25] Again Gompers used Wright to approach Spargo about terminating his plans to create another loyalty movement. Wright asked Spargo to declare whether he planned to remain in the Alliance or direct his own organization.[26]

23. Gaylord to Gompers, Oct. 11, 1917, Gompers papers.
24. Chester Wright to Gaylord, Oct. 13, 1917, copy, C.P.I. papers, 1-A5-1; Gaylord to Gompers, Oct. 12, 16, 1917, Gompers papers.
25. Gompers to Maisel, Sept. 29, 1917, Gompers papers.
26. Wright to Spargo, Oct. 2, 1917, *ibid.*

Spargo, however, had no intention of stating his plans and he curtly shot back, "The Alliance should attend to its own ample business."[27]

Shortly thereafter Spargo, Stokes, and Matthew Hale, a progressive of Boston, led the call for a third party convention in Chicago. This convention was to discuss the establishment of a new radical group which would declare its loyalty to the Administration, yet remain liberal in ideology. But the factionalism which often plagued American liberalism threatened to disrupt Spargo's plans. Although records of this Chicago convention are sparse, it is apparent that there was little agreement among those present as to the value of such a party. Spargo urged those attending to accept the new movement because the Alliance was too closely tied to the Democratic party and the A.F. of L. for radical autonomy.[28] There was agreement that Spargo's charges were justifiable, but there was little agreement as to how the party should be formed. The result of Spargo's effort was an agreement to set up the National party; however, it was apparent that the organization would have serious defects. Clarence Darrow and Robert Maisel, who had been in Chicago spying on the meeting for the Alliance, reported back: "It is nothing but a joke . . . nothing will come of this. They are now debating whether to recognize God." Maisel observed that "God missed out on the platform but got in the preamble by a close shave."[29]

Hearing that the Chicago convention was less than a success, Gompers asked Maisel to see if Spargo would now drop his dualist plans. But again Spargo refused to knuckle under to Gompers' demands and retorted, "Since the Alliance is non-partisan I can do what I please in political actions";[30] whereupon Maisel urged Gompers to denounce the National party.[31] Chester Wright had second thoughts on the matter. Although he had been accused by Spargo of "fighting us under cover,"[32] he mildly labeled the dis-

27. Spargo to Wright, telegram, Oct. 4, 1917, copy, C.P.I. papers, 1-A5.
28. Maisel to Gompers, Oct. 11, 1917, Gompers papers. There is some material on the Chicago meeting in the Stokes papers, Box 28, including a copy of Spargo's speech, Oct. 4, 1917.
29. Maisel to Gompers, Oct. 5, 1917; Maisel to Gompers, telegram, Oct. 6, 1917, Gompers papers.
30. Spargo to Gompers, Oct. 9, 1917, *ibid.*
31. Maisel to Gompers, Oct. 11, 1917, C.P.I. papers, 1-A5.
32. Spargo to Wright, Oct. 12, 1917, Stokes papers, Box 28.

agreement "a misunderstanding which would clear up in time if the Alliance were only patient."[33] For his part, Spargo had had enough of Gompers' meddling and threatened to resign from the Alliance if he were not allowed "to be my own boss."[34] By now Gompers realized that Spargo was seriously upset; for fear of splitting the Alliance he decided to tolerate Spargo's dualism in the belief that the National party would fail.[35]

The differences between Spargo and Gompers were not the only difficulties which threatened the Alliance. The relationship between the Alliance and its sponsor, the C.P.I., was strained from the beginning because neither Creel nor Maisel had worked out clear-cut lines of authority. Creel seldom understood Maisel's need for funds; and, because he was not aware of the scarcity of money among the unions, Creel was constantly urging Maisel to raise more funds from the A.F. of L.'s unions.[36] Maisel attempted many times to solicit donations from the Federation but never succeeded in raising more than a few hundred dollars at a time.[37] This left the Alliance totally dependent on Creel's resources. Creel was suspicious that the Alliance was not doing all that it could to raise money. After one turbulent meeting Maisel complained to Gompers, "I feel hurt after the talk with Creel. You know that the Alliance needs much money. . . ."[38] Convinced that the labor movement could do more to finance its own loyalty work, Creel ordered his staff to cease paying the Alliance's debts except for those pertaining to salaries and rents. Everything else, he declared, was to be paid by Maisel.[39]

Creel's attitude toward finances can also be explained as a result of some criticism from Congress over evidences of mismanagement within the C.P.I. The criticism had started when the C.P.I. allowed some midwestern German-language newspapers, which were publishing Alliance-C.P.I. propaganda, to print whatever they wished. Senator Paul O. Hustings of Wisconsin had read

33. Wright to Gompers, Oct. 13, 1917, Gompers papers.
34. Spargo to Wright, Oct. 16, 1917, Stokes papers, Box 28.
35. Wright to Gompers, Oct. 18, 1917, Gompers papers.
36. Financial report, American Alliance, undated copy, C.P.I. papers, 1-A6.
37. For the few remaining financial statements of the American Alliance, see Stokes papers, Boxes 27-31.
38. Maisel to Gompers, Oct. 5, 1917, Gompers papers.
39. Creel to Chaffey, Sept. 21, 1917, C.P.I. papers, 1-A5.

what he considered "pro-German" statements in the columns of these papers, and he advised Wilson of this fact. Creel was asked to explain why these papers were not being censored. Shortly thereafter they were dropped from the C.P.I.'s favored list.[40] But this was only part of the problem. The Senate soon began an extensive investigation of the C.P.I. which revealed a large amount of fiscal waste. In the midst of this investigation, Creel tightened up his expenditures and acted with extreme caution to avoid further criticism. Consequently, the Alliance was caught in an economy squeeze as Creel cut back on some of the funds that he originally had set aside for the Alliance's use.[41]

With its program weakened because of these C.P.I. cutbacks, Maisel found himself hampered seriously in his efforts to oppose Council propaganda. And when the Council began its campaign to organize the East Side, Maisel was unable to oppose the pacifists effectively. At times the garment workers were so stirred by the Council's propaganda that they disrupted several Alliance rallies.[42] Smarting from these reverses, Maisel complained bitterly to Gompers that the Alliance needed to step up its "loyalty" crusade on the East Side. "But Creel," he observed, "does not seem to realize that money is involved!"[43] The situation worsened when Council organizers moved deeper into the garment industry with several sound trucks which drove about blaring anti-war propaganda. The Council was doing such a good job at propagandizing against the war that the loyal Jewish Socialist League feared the entire East Side would go over to the pacifists;[44] Maisel lamented, "The *Forward* crowd is reporting that even the government is afraid of them!"[45]

Alliance officials hurriedly searched for some way to pacify the East Side. But their program had to be conducted with a minimum of funds, and it was impossible for a major loyalty effort to be

40. Creel to Tumulty, Sept. 19, 1917, Wilson papers.
41. Byoir to Maisel, Oct. 25, 1917, C.P.I. papers, 1-A6; Chaffey to Creel, Sept. 27, 1917, *ibid.*, 1-A5; Wright to Gompers, Oct. 5, 1917, Gompers papers. In November, Congress completed one investigation of the C.P.I. and charged it with financial extravagance (Cronon, ed., *Cabinet Diaries*, p. 465).
42. Chyken to Maisel, Oct. 6, 1917, C.P.I. papers, 1-A6.
43. Maisel to Gompers, Oct. 10, 1917, *ibid.*
44. Maisel to Gompers, Oct. 17, 1917, Gompers papers.
45. Maisel to Gompers, Oct. 18, 1917, *ibid.*

organized. It was decided to stage a series of Liberty Loan rallies
with a battery of volunteer speakers who were to cover the East
Side.[46] The Council had created a tense situation there, and to
protect Alliance speakers from violence, Gompers asked his old
friend Ernest Bohm to call out his Central Federated Union members to police the crowds who attended the rallies.[47] The plan
worked beautifully: Alliance speakers were unmolested and the
relatively inexpensive Liberty Loan rallies proved to be a practical
way to work with a minimum of expense. The East Side campaign
pacified the area for the moment.[48] Since the Liberty Loan rallies
worked well in this instance, the Alliance conducted a series of
them throughout the country. In James Maurer's stronghold of
Pittsburgh a successful loan rally was held which attracted large
numbers of socialists.[49] Other rallies were successfully held in Kansas, Michigan, and California.[50]

While the Alliance struggled to maintain itself on a tight budget, the Peoples Council attempted to get its own national program
under way. But it faced problems as serious as those which con-
fronted the Alliance. The Council's chief problem lay not so much
in its lack of funds, but with the success of the nation's loyal
press, the Wilson Administration, and the Alliance in branding
the movement as extremist. To many Americans the council movement seemed but the echo of German peace propaganda enthu-
siasts who were bent on gaining a negotiated peace. Likewise,
when the Council endorsed the Bolshevik peace proposals, many
people associated the group with all the connotations of Bolshevism. The Council intended no violent overthrow of the American
government and had proclaimed its desire to keep within the
moderate philosophy of American socialism;[51] yet the non-revolu-
tionary nature of the movement never came across to many Americans who were becoming fearful of liberals, socialists, and mal-
contents who opposed the Wilson Administration. The Council's

46. Maisel to Gompers, Oct. 19, 1917, *ibid.*
47. Bohm to Gompers, Oct. 22, 1917, *ibid.*
48. Maisel to Gompers, Oct. 20, 1917, *ibid.*
49. Maisel to Gompers, Oct. 28, 1917, *ibid.*
50. Progress report, American Alliance, Oct. 25, 1917, *ibid.*
51. Peterson and Fite, *Opponents of War*, p. 76; Fine, *Labor and Farmers' Parties*, p. 337. The left wing of the party was attacking the moderates
at this time for being allied with the Council, which they believed too mild.

image as a radical organization suffered further when former Senator John Works resigned over what he considered the increasingly radical outlook of the organization's leadership. Works referred especially to Scott Nearing, who had spoken for revolution if political action failed to achieve the Council's programs.[52]

As was the case with the Alliance, the initial task of the Council was finding sufficient funds to operate its programs. This delicate task fell upon the able shoulders of James Maurer, the robust leader of Pennsylvania labor. Maurer ran into difficulties immediately when he issued a call to those responsible for raising funds to meet him in Chicago. The Midwest was proving to be increasingly hostile toward the Council because of Gaylord's efforts and a vicious pro-war campaign directed by the Chicago press. Upon receiving reports that the Council meeting in Chicago would attract adverse publicity, Maurer ordered the delegates to travel to the national headquarters in New York City where the first order of business would be to erase the debt created by the national convention and to assure the Council of a continuous income. To accomplish this objective, Maurer suggested that only those unafraid to associate openly with the movement take an active position on the financial committee. (Maurer's suggestion was well taken; the Baltimore headquarters of the Council had just been raided by the local police.)[53] If any member, Maurer asserted, were hesitant to be identified with the movement or was too busy to take on the responsibility of raising funds, he might contribute secretly.[54]

Again adversity struck the Council when it became known that Count Johann-Heinrich von Bernstorff, the pre-war German ambassador at Washington, had had $50,000 at his disposal to spend on German propaganda in the United States. When this news broke, some Americans believed that this money had been spent by the Socialist party to spread German propaganda at the last minute to prevent the country from entering the war. Although the New York *Call* declared that Bernstorff had given the money to certain congressmen to vote against the war, its editorials failed to con-

---

52. Frederick L. Paxson, *America at War* (Boston, 1939), II, 55.
53. New York *Call*, Sept. 11, 1917; Executive Committee report, P.C.A., Sept. 10, 1917, Swarthmore.
54. Executive Committee report, P.C.A., Sept. 16, 1917, Swarthmore.

vince much public opinion.[55] The entire episode added further circumstantial evidence that the Council, as the socialists' ally, was too a "pro-German" movement. Consequently the Council's efforts to raise money from American moderates fell flat. Since the pacifists themselves were far from wealthy, their campaign failed to provide the needed funds. By October their treasury showed a deficit.

New and more drastic measures were needed to finance the movement, and a bold plan to bill each member for a period of ten months was adopted. At the same time, the Council withdrew its contributions to the Socialist Legal Aid Society, an organization formed to defend radicals jailed for sedition.[56] To supplement the dues system, Council chapters in each state were assessed a membership fee based on their size and wealth.[57] The success of these plans was demonstrated when the Council pulled its finances out of the red by November.[58] Maurer was especially elated over this scheme because the Council was able to boast that, unlike the Alliance, it existed on the voluntary donations of its members.[59]

Whether the Council could continue to obtain sufficient funds was open to question. It was apparent in September when Morris Hillquit resigned as chairman to enter the New York mayoralty race that a much needed moderating element was gone. The fact that Scott Nearing, "a noted radical" as the *Call* praised him, took over the office and introduced a more extreme program only promised to make the Council's position even more difficult.[60] Recent police intervention already had prevented the carrying out of several Council rallies in the East, including one in Pittsburgh which had been broken up before it had started. Added to this the dismissal of Professor H. W. L. Dana of Columbia University

55. New York *Call*, Sept. 22, 1917. Bernstorff apparently was to spend the money in the national press and perhaps give some to his agents. It is not known exactly how he spent the money. However, there is no record that the Socialist party or the Council received a cent.
56. Executive Committee report, P.C.A. Oct. 16, 1917, Swarthmore.
57. P.C.A. *Bulletin*, Vol. I, No. 6, Oct. 24, 1917, Tamiment Institute; Nearing to Dana, Oct. 18, 1917, Dana papers.
58. Nearing, P.C.A. circular, Oct. 31, 1917, Swarthmore.
59. Maurer had asked Gompers earlier the embarrassing question of who paid the Alliance's bills (New York *Call*, Oct. 7, 1917).
60. *Ibid.*, Sept. 23, 1917; New York *Times*, Sept. 20, 1917.

for his Council activities had made headlines in many eastern papers.[61] Moreover, the Council was threatened with losing its headquarters because its landlord was being heckled by his pro-war friends for leasing the building to the pacifists.[62] Despite these problems, Nearing continued to speak out for extremism. His statements only frightened many into believing that the council movement was a threat to the American way of life.[63]

Nearing's temperament clashed with that of Lochner, who had been an ardent follower of Hillquit. A power struggle soon got under way within the Executive Committee between Nearing's friends, who wanted a more belligerent movement, and Lochner's supporters, who wished to maintain a moderate approach. Since Nearing was the better known of the two, Lochner saw little hope of keeping the movement moderate. Therefore he submitted his resignation to the Executive Committee; but the committee contained more moderates than liberals and rejected the resignation.[64] Jane Addams, who watched these events from Chicago, wrote to David Starr Jordan, "The situation and membership is confused with good people and self-seekers."[65] With the moderates exercising a larger degree of power, the committee worked out a compromise between the two factions. Nearing would continue to direct the Council, but each member of the Executive Committee hereafter would vote by secret ballot on every policy decision; a majority of dissenting ballots would force a policy change. Elated over the compromise, Lochner wrote Jordan about the Council's "new democratic organization."[66]

Shortly after Nearing took over leadership of the Council movement, the Wilson Administration began a severe crackdown on espionage and sedition. The government's program was directed by Attorney General Thomas W. Gregory. As the Council struggled to make its voice heard throughout the land, it had been

61. New York *Call*, Sept. 28, 29, 1917.
62. New York *Times*, Sept. 22, 1917.
63. *Ibid.*, Oct. 2, 1917. Nearing said that the Council afforded the only real opportunity to work for peace, as well as its being a clearinghouse for radicals. On October 10 he was barred from speaking in Cincinnati (New York *Call*, Oct. 11, 1917).
64. Executive Committee report, P.C.A., Oct. 2, 1917, Swarthmore.
65. Addams to Jordan, Oct. 2, 1917, Jordan papers.
66. Lochner to Jordan, Oct. 23, 1917, *ibid.*

labeled by the Justice Department a seditious organization.[67] When Council officials had heard that they were a target of the government's ire, they had offered to open their files to any governmental official searching for seditious material.[68] The Justice Department had ignored this offer, however, and on October 6 the Council headquarters in Chicago had been raided along with that of the Socialist party. Shortly thereafter the nation's foremost radical newspapers had been ordered into court to declare any reasons why they should not be barred from the mails. The offices of the *Volksblatt*, a German-American paper, had been raided, and the *Forward* had been charged with publishing seditious material.[69] At the same time Max Eastman's *Masses* had been ordered into court on the same charges, and the socialist *Volkszeitung*, the most influential German-language paper in the country, had been indicted.[70] The charge against the New York *Call* however, was the most serious to the Council and to the Socialist party.

The government's threat to ban the *Call* from the mails produced one of the largest protest rallies ever seen at Madison Square Garden. Sponsored by the Socialist party and supported by a number of anti-war societies, including the Council, the rally drew more than 35,000 people to hear Morris Hillquit, then in the midst of his mayoralty race, James Maurer, and Scott Nearing bitterly accuse the government of banning free speech. Even Eugene Debs, who had remained in the Midwest throughout all the turmoil, wired his support of the rally.[71]

The Administration's stern suppression of the pacifist publications touched off protests from coast to coast. William Bross Lloyd, a socialist and Council member, sent numerous telegrams to the White House demanding that Wilson allow freedom of expression at home while the country was fighting for democracy abroad.[72] The influential editor of the *New Republic*, Herbert

67. P.C.A. *Bulletin*, Vol. I, No. 5, Sept. 13, 1917, Tamiment Institute.
68. Lochner to Attorney General Gregory, Sept. 10, 1917, Swarthmore.
69. New York *Times*, Oct. 7, 1917.
70. Max Eastman, *Reflections on the Failure of Socialism* (New York, 1955), pp. 9-10; New York *Call*, Oct. 9, 1917. Eastman gives a short account of the origin of the *Masses* in his book.
71. New York *Call*, Oct. 15, 1917.
72. William B. Lloyd to Wilson, telegram, Oct. 19, 1917, Wilson papers. There are numerous telegrams of a similar nature from Lloyd in the Wilson papers.

Croly, joined in the protests by urging the President to use persuasion rather than suppression to do away with sedition.[73] In California, Upton Sinclair asked Wilson to stop his personal suppression of the socialist press and set up an impartial information bureau to censor the news.[74]

The Administration's suppression of the radical press hurt the Council's efforts to distribute its propaganda; thus, a new voluntary distribution system was immediately started. In October, Council officials ordered their locals to distribute propaganda by going from door to door if necessary. The material was to be placed at distribution centers throughout the country. Each local was told to appoint someone to go to these centers, pick up the propaganda material, and carry it back to their chapters. Other members were given the jobs of carrying the propaganda from Council headquarters in New York to these distribution points.[75] In this way Council officials hoped to avoid censorship and save some much needed money on postage.

While the Council was engaged in its struggle against censorship, other issues captured its interest. These were the climax of Hillquit's campaign to become mayor of New York, and Jacob Panken's effort to obtain a judgeship on the East side. Hillquit had decided to oppose an independent Democrat, John P. Mitchel, and the regular Democratic party candidate, John F. Hylan of Brooklyn, in a contest, which if not victorious for the socialists, would at least allow them to air their grievances against the Democratic party.[76] To strengthen Hillquit's campaign, Nearing urged Council members to aid the Socialist party in every way possible.[77]

Hillquit and Panken had a large following among New York's Jewish elements and a great deal of emotion was manifest during the Campaign. More than twenty thousand people gathered in

73. Herbert Croly to Wilson, Oct. 19, 1917, *ibid.*
74. Upton Sinclair to Wilson, Oct. 22, 1917, *ibid.*
75. Executive Committee circular, P.C.A., Oct. 3, 1917, Swarthmore; Nearing to all Council members, Oct. 8, 1917, *ibid.*; unsigned memorandum, Woman's Peace Party, Sept. 24, 1917, *ibid.* This memorandum expressed the willingness of the party to distribute Council propaganda.
76. Hillquit, *Loose Leaves*, p. 180; New York *Call*, Oct. 7, 1917; New York *Times*, Oct. 7, 1917.
77. Nearing to all secretaries, Oct. 31, 1917, Swarthmore.

Madison Square Garden to demonstrate their support for the candidates, while some fifty thousand workers marched for the ticket on the East Side.[78] Hillquit made a dramatic appearance before the loyal Jewish Socialist League but created such a stir between the anti- and pro-war factions present that even the pleas of the Alliance's Jacob Chykin failed to preserve order. The meeting broke up in complete confusion.[79]

Hillquit's campaign also attracted wide interest outside New York City. From the Midwest, Eugene Debs wired, "I wish I could be there to fight it too."[80] But some of the most intense interest came from Democratic party leaders, who feared that Hillquit might win some of the normally Democratic votes. Moreover, the Democrats were especially fearful that a large socialist vote might be interpreted as a protest against the Wilson Administration's war policies.[81] The strongest campaign statements were not made by Administration officials, however, but by former President Theodore Roosevelt who charged Hillquit with being a pacifist coward who attracted a coward's vote.[82]

There was no time when the Democratic party bosses in New York City took Hillquit's candidacy seriously, but their feverish activity against him was to prevent the Socialist party from becoming a disturbing influence in New York politics. As was expected, a record vote was counted and Hillquit lost. It was significant, however, that despite the Administration's efforts to prevent a large socialist turnout, Hillquit polled the greatest socialist vote in years, gaining more than five times as many votes as any previous socialist mayoral candidate. Panken was more fortunate and easily won his East Side judgeship.[83] One significant result of the elections was the failure of the government's loyalty campaign to stem the anti-war feeling in New York City.

78. New York *Call*, Sept. 24, 1917.
79. *Ibid.*, Oct. 6, 1917.
80. Debs to Hillquit, Sept. 21, 1917, Hillquit papers, State Historical Society of Wisconsin, Madison.
81. New York *Call*, Oct. 30, 1917.
82. Hillquit, *Loose Leaves*, pp. 183, 193.
83. New York *Times*, Oct. 30, 1917; Hillquit, *Loose Leaves*, p. 206; New York *Call*, Nov. 7, 1917. Hillquit received 145,332 votes and ran third, trailing Mitchel. The winning candidate, Hylan, received 313,956 votes.

The early fall months had been a trying time for the Alliance and the Council. The initial problems involved in establishing their national programs had furnished both organizations with a series of difficulties concerning finances, and for the Council, government censorship. Each organization had extended its influence, and both were determined to continue their efforts to win over labor. As for the Alliance, it had aided the government by holding the A.F. of L. firmly behind the war effort during the critical months after America's entry into the war. Gompers believed that this had done much to prevent labor obstructionism during the period, thereby allowing the country to mobilize more effectively the war effort.[84] Although the Alliance was loosely organized, riddled with strife, and badly in need of funds, it was the symbol of conservative labor's determination to remain loyal at a time when thousands of vocal pacifists were calling America's participation in the war a "capitalistic adventure."

Chapter 6. The Renaissance of Pacifism and the Misuse of Labor Loyalty

In November Gompers turned his attention primarily to directing the A.F. of L.'s wartime program, serving on the Council of National Defense, and doing those numerous other jobs which made his life a whirl of conferences and travel. The Alliance was left to Maisel's direction since obstructionism in labor appeared to be of little threat after the Council had failed to capture initially the imagination of the American worker. As the A.F. of L.'s "loyalty" watchdog agency, the Alliance had only to oppose any further pacifist labor propaganda. Gompers hoped that he could now devote his full time to building a powerful labor movement and leave problems of loyalty to Maisel.

But as the American people had learned in 1914, all the decisions which influenced their lives were not made in Washington, D.C. From socialist Russia came the disturbing news that the Bolsheviks had succeeded in revolting against the Kerenski gov-

---

84. Gompers, *Seventy Years*, II, 384. Gompers believed that the tide of pacifism had been turned by the autumn of 1917.

ernment and that civil war had broken out.¹ The days passed, during which it became clear that the Bolsheviks were directing a well-planned revolution that was a threat to the Russian war effort. The implications became ominous to the Wilson Administration, for the Bolsheviks long had advocated a separate peace with Germany. If Russia left the war, the Allies would have to face an additional one million German troops on the western front at a time when the United States was still hurrying to dispatch its first large troop commitments to Europe. To increase the seriousness of the situation, the Bolsheviks had called on the working classes of the world to rise up against their capitalistic governments and form a world socialist community. The very fact that the Bolsheviks were succeeding in doing this in Russia seemed to many to make other revolutions imminent in Europe and perhaps in the United States.

As a result, in America radicalism and the fear of radicalism were rekindled. No one in November, 1917, knew just what effect the Russian revolution would have upon America's socialists or upon the council movement which had been loud in its praise of the Bolsheviks. Radicals like John Reed, a Council member and one of America's most controversial journalists, were thrilled that a nation of one hundred million had been snatched from "the clutches of an imperialistic war. . . ."² Moreover, many left-wing labormen, like William Z. Foster, who was at this time a member of the A.F. of L., could exclaim that the revolution was "the labor movement carried to its logical conclusion . . . ," as well as a new day for the worker who had depended on "the American Federation of Labor's lackluster affairs . . ." to represent his wishes.³

The immediate result of the revolution, however, was not to touch off a workers' revolt in America, but to strengthen those left-wingers in the council movement and the Socialist party who

1. Bernard Pares, *History of Russia* (New York, 1947), pp. 474-475; Edward H. Carr, *The Bolsheviki Revolution* (New York, 1951), I, 105-123.
2. John Stuart, *The Education of John Reed* (New York, 1955), p. 28. For Reed's account of the Russian Revolution, see *Ten Days That Shook the World* (New York, 1935).
3. William Z. Foster, *The Russian Revolution* (New York, 1955), pp. 6, 45.

had ardently supported the Bolsheviks.[4] Alexander Trachtenberg, a former tsarist soldier, a Council member, and a prominent lecturer for the socialists, immediately proclaimed his support of the revolution; while the New York *Call* applauded the Bolsheviks because they had upset the Kerenski government with a minimum of bloodshed.[5] Generally, America's radical elements chose to wait on events as they unfolded within Russia.

The President reacted quickly after the revolution. He held several conferences with Colonel House, who advised him to formulate a war aims program before the Bolsheviks succeeded in driving Russia from the war. Already the chorus at home of those calling for America to declare her war objectives was growing increasingly louder. Wilson was now in an awkward position: he was forced to pacify the Russian people so as to keep them in the war, and at the same time he was putting down extremism at home.[6]

The news that the Bolsheviks were revolting against the Kerenski government revitalized the Peoples Council movement. Whereas radicalism had appeared on the wane in late October, the pacifists now took new hope from the revolution and rekindled their efforts to pressure Wilson to accept the Bolsheviks as Russia's legitimate rulers; they hurriedly organized more campaigns to force Wilson to forsake his support of this "capitalistic war." And if the government failed to heed their pressure? They pointedly observed that a government which blocked the expression of its people's will would go the way of the Kerenski regime.[7] Plans were formulated to organize pacifist cells in America's colleges so as to build a hard core of intellectuals who could use the students' inquiring minds to agitate for peace.[8] For the masses, however, the Rand School in New York City prepared classes on socialism, pacifism, and the responsibilities of internationalism. H. W. D. Dana, recently fired from Columbia University for his radicalism, accepted a lectureship here, as did Scott Nearing and Alexander Trachtenberg.[9]

4. Bell, "Background and Development," pp. 319-320.
5. New York *Call*, Nov. 9, 10, 1917.
6. Charles Seymour, ed., *The Intimate Papers of Colonel House* (New York, 1926), III, 317; Bell, "Background and Development," pp. 320-321.
7. P.C.A. news release, Nov. 1917, copy, Swarthmore.
8. Nearing to Dana, Nov. 17, 1917, Dana papers.
9. New York *Call*, Nov. 11, 1917.

The aggressiveness of the Council's renewed peace offensive was soon apparent. At Cooper Union the Alliance's J. G. Phelps Stokes was heckled from the stage by a loud group of agitators who strongly challenged Wilson's right to lead the American people.[10] The next day the Council's Executive Committee announced a revised program for peace and "industrial democracy," which included the nationalization of all production, adequate compensation to workers for their labor, and the establishment of an international brotherhood to ensure the peace.[11] A week later Council members were urged to demand that their congressmen support America's withdrawal from the war when Bolshevik Russia withdrew. Moreover, sympathy and support were extended to a new radical society called the Friends of Russia, which contained Crystal Eastman and Trachtenberg as members. On December 3, when the Friends held one of their first rallies demanding recognition of the Bolsheviks, these Council members were much in evidence.[12]

Earlier in Seattle, Council pacifists had completely disrupted a local Alliance rally, and reports from the Midwest had indicated a sudden upsurge of pacifism in that area;[13] in California, Council locals had made new plans for more peace rallies similar to those held during the summer in Los Angeles and San Francisco.[14] Back in New York the Executive Committee had reported a sharp increase in the *Bulletin*'s circulation, and several leftist theater groups had been established at the Rand School.[15]

Council members had been cheered on in their work when John Reed, who had gone to Russia to observe the revolution, wired back greetings from the Russian Workingmen's Councils; and when Lord Lansdowne, a former British secretary of war and foreign affairs, had called upon his government to accept the Bolsheviks' peace proposals.[16] But in England Fabian socialist

10. *Ibid.*, Nov. 13, 1917.
11. *Ibid.*, Nov. 14, 1917.
12. *Ibid.*, Dec. 5, 1917.
13. Frank Gatis to Gompers, Nov. 5, 1917, Gompers papers.
14. William Short to Jordan, Nov. 8, 1917, Jordan papers.
15. Executive Committee report, P.C.A., Nov. 8, 1917, Swarthmore; P.C.A. *Bulletin*, Vol. I, No. 9, Nov. 11, 1917, *ibid.*; New York *Times*, Nov. 18, 1917; New York *Call*, Nov. 22, 1917.
16. New York *Call*, Nov. 22, 1917.

Beatrice Webb bemoaned the fact that Wilson would not instruct Gompers to link up with the world socialist movement to form a coalition against the imperialists of the world.[17] The Council took every advantage of this renewed ferment for peace by charging that Wilson personally wanted peace but was completely under the control of Wall Street munition barons. To stress this point, Nearing wrote a series of open letters to the New York *Times* asking why America was so steadfastly committed to the total defeat of Germany if she desired nothing but peace from the war.[18] But perhaps the most powerful propaganda used by the Council at this time was supplied by the Bolsheviks themselves, when they released the publicly unknown terms of the secret treaties made among the Allies. Although concluded before the American declaration of war in April, 1917, these treaties showed that America's associates were interested in exploiting a victory for selfish reasons.[19]

Against this background Elizabeth Freeman declared "the peace movement is not dead!" and Hillquit wrote of the urgent need for a socialist-inspired peace treaty. William Bross Lloyd, speaking in Chicago on "Peace, Now You See It—Now You Don't," cried out dramatically to his audience, "The Bolsheviks are calling you, they are working for an immediate armistice. Are you there? Do your part!"[20]

The intensification of the pacifist propaganda campaign caused profound concern in Washington where Postmaster Burleson, fearing an increased use of the mails for seditious purposes, wrote Creel that "the present situation presents a problem which appears to me serious in the extreme. . . ."[21] But the most spectacular action taken by the Administration had been President Wilson's decision to accept an invitation to appear before the A.F.

17. P.C.A. *Bulletin*, Vol. I, No. 11, Dec. 14, 1917, Swarthmore; Margaret Cole, ed., *Beatrice Webb's Diary* (London, 1952), I, 114.

18. "Who Get the Profits?" P.C.A. pamphlet, copy, Tamiment Institute; "Germany Wants Peace and Disarmament," P.C.A., Swarthmore; Scott Nearing, "Open Letters to Profiteers," *ibid*.

19. "Secret Diplomacy and Profiteering," P.C.A. publication, *ibid*.

20. Elizabeth Freeman to co-workers, Dec. 20, 1917, *ibid*.; Hillquit to William Ward, Dec. 20, 1917, Hillquit papers; William Bross Lloyd, speech, Chicago, Dec. 21, 1917, Swarthmore.

21. Burleson to Creel, Dec. 10, 1917, Postmaster General's papers, National Archives.

of L.'s annual convention at Buffalo.[22] Gompers' invitation to Wilson had been considered necessary for two reasons. Foremost in his mind had been the building of a respectable image for the A.F. of L. But Gompers had also faced some severe criticism from those dissident elements within the A.F. of L. who were challenging his close co-operation with capitalism and his willingness to go along with Wilson's demands for total victory.[23] Among these dissident elements were hundreds of Council pacifists who had charged that Gompers was unscrupulous,[24] but still "one of the brilliant opponents of the Peoples Council movement."[25]

The convention had opened in a flurry of excitement as President and Mrs. Wilson had entered the Hall with a cortege of soldiers and had taken their seats on the platform beside Gompers. As the President rose to speak, thousands of delegates gave him a standing ovation. Wilson's speech was especially hard-hitting, containing his usual eloquent phrases which he skilfully directed at those who demanded a cessation of the war. The war would not end short of total victory, the President declared, and any other plan to that effect was "as fatuous as the framers of Russia."[26] Although he refused to provide a precise declaration of America's war aims at this time, it was clear to those present that the President did not intend to endorse those of the Bolsheviks. Wilson continued in his characteristic prose, outlining for the delegates the reasons for the war as he saw them.[27]

The President then turned to more immediate matters and spoke of labor's essential role in the winning of the war through fewer strikes and work stoppages. But it was his emphatic endorsement of Gompers' leadership that was unprecedented: "If I may be permitted to do so I want to express my admiration of his

22. Baker, *Woodrow Wilson: Life and Letters,* VII, 350; Gompers to the press, Nov. 10, 1917, Gompers papers.
23. New York *Call,* Nov. 12, 1917. The *Call* declared that the A.F. of L.'s pacifists were preparing for "a freedom fight."
24. *Ibid.,* Nov. 14, 1917.
25. *Ibid.,* Nov. 18, 1917.
26. *Report of Proceedings,* A. F. of L., 37th annual convention, Buffalo, Nov. 12-24, 1917 (Washington, D.C., 1917), pp. 1-2.
27. Lansing believed that the State Department's policy at this stage should be one of watchful waiting concerning the Bolshevik Revolution "until the black period of terrorism has come to an end. . ." Lansing, confidential notebook, II, Dec. 2, 7, 1917, Robert Lansing memoranda, Library of Congress.

[Gompers'] patriotic courage, his large vision, and his statesman-like sense of what has to be done." When the President stepped back from the lectern, the delegates rose to their feet and led by Gompers gave three rousing cheers for this man who had held the A.F. of L.'s support since 1912. Mrs. Wilson cordially received a large bouquet of American Beauty roses, and after shaking hands with the A.F. of L.'s leaders Wilson and the First Lady left the hall for Washington.

The President's appearance at Buffalo had left no doubt of the Administration's approval of the Federation. Maisel optimistically had written to Creel that the President's visit "would kill entirely" the pacifists' plans to challenge the A.F. of L.; but he concluded, "They are still on the lookout, however, and some trouble may turn up. . . ."[28]

After the President's departure, the delegates had settled down to approving a series of resolutions concerning the A.F. of L.'s war-time policies, one of which called for an endorsement by the rank-and-file of the American Alliance for Labor and Democracy. As was expected, the Alliance resolution had touched off a pacifist attack on the moderates. Led by J. Mahlon Barnes of the International Cigar Makers Union and James H. Fisher of Montana, a small group of determined socialists had fired question after question at Gompers about the need for the Alliance.[29] Barnes had asked why the A.F. of L. found it necessary to "Americanize American labor?" If the Alliance really expressed the will of the rank-and-file, he asserted, why did it approve Wilson's censorship policies, and why did it not stand up for labor's just demands? Gompers had been clearly angered by Barnes's questions, but the old chief had not survived decades of criticism without learning how to debate the opposition. Characteristically, Gompers had answered some questions, others he had ignored. He had assured Barnes and Fisher that the Alliance did represent the views of the majority of the A.F. of L.'s unions, and that no one had been more concerned with labor's just demands than he. The debate had continued for more than an hour. But the crafty old parliamentarian had successfully put aside both personal insults and socialist

28. Maisel to Creel, Nov. 16, 1917, C.P.I. papers, 1-A1-26. *Report of Proceedings*, A. F. of L., gives the full text of the President's speech.
29. New York *Call*, Nov. 21, 1917.

propaganda, and, finally tiring of the debate, had called for a vote on an endorsement of the Alliance. The members had followed Gompers' leadership and had voted 21,602 to 402 in favor of endorsing the Alliance as the A.F. of L.'s official loyalty agency.[30]

After his loyal stand at Buffalo, the *Times* had loudly acclaimed Gompers for working "hand in hand with the Administration." But the New York *Call* had remarked that Gompers deserved this praise only because "certain large unions could not afford to break this year with the Administration." The *Call* editor had predicted that another attack on the A.F. of L.'s "pro-governmental leadership" would follow at the next convention in St. Paul.[31] Gompers, for his part, had praised the A.F. of L.'s endorsement of the loyalty program and had answered the *Call*'s charges by declaring that "there was a direct line of communication between Petrograd and certain socialist radicals in New York City."[32]

After Wilson's dramatic endorsement of the A.F. of L. and the Alliance, and in response to the current upsurge in pacifism, the Alliance unleashed a renewed attack against labor obstructionism by distributing a series of hard-hitting loyalty pamphlets, some of them written by the famous Wisconsin economist John R. Commons. Commons had been commissioned by the C.P.I. to write the series to defend the Administration against charges that it was exploiting labor during the war. If labor opposed the Administration's policies, Commons asserted in one of these, Germany was sure to win the war and the world labor movement would be set back a hundred years. But there was no reason to believe that the workingman was being exploited, he declared, for business was more heavily taxed by the Wilson Administration than was the entire American public.[33]

In another pamphlet, "Why the War Must Be Won," an anonymous C.P.I. writer proclaimed that Wilson's peace program would attain the aims of organized labor if labor would only prove its responsibility in aiding the war effort. In "I Solemnly

30. *Report of Proceedings*, A. F. of L., pp. 283-308.
31. New York *Times*, Nov. 20, 1917; New York *Call*, Nov. 25, 1917.
32. "The Kaiser's Secret Army Here," *Literary Digest*, LV (Dec. 1, 1917), 15-16; New York *Times*, Nov. 30, 1917.
33. John R. Commons, "Why Workmen Support the War" and "Who Is Paying for the War?" C.P.I. publications, Gompers papers.

Promise," another writer urged the worker to continue his support of Wilson because the A.F. of L. would "impress the American public with its loyalty."[34] No phrase was left unturned in these pamphlets to point out to the laborer that if he failed to support the war effort he would lose a golden opportunity to ingratiate himself with the nation.

Shortly after the Buffalo convention the Alliance became involved in a quarrel with the United Hebrew Trades and Sidney Hillman's Amalgamated Clothing Workers of America. This dispute was, in actuality, the reopening of an older one dating back to December, 1914, when Hillman had bolted the A.F. of L.'s United Garment Workers of America and had set up his own union. The Amalgamated was a success and soon had organized more than forty thousand garment workers along industrial trade lines. Hillman also gained the support of the powerful United Hebrew Trades, an organization of Jewish workers formed in the late 1880's, which sympathized with the liberal attitude of the Amalgamated. Indeed, the Trades had supported Hillman and turned its back on the A.F. of L.'s United Garment Workers, which was against industrial unionism and, consequently, a rival of the Amalgamated. Feeling that the Amalgamated and the Trades were hampering its efforts to "Americanize" labor on the East Side, the Alliance sought every opportunity to discredit both rivals.

There was no denying that both organizations were riddled with pacifists, Council members, and socialists. The general secretary of the Amalgamated, Benjamin Schlossberg, and the president of the United Hebrew Trades, Max Pine, were members of the council movement. And although Hillman himself never joined the movement, he tolerated anyone in his union who agreed with its personal brand of liberalism. To make matters worse for Gompers, the president of the International Garment Workers Union, Benjamin Schlesinger, was a socialist, a Council member, and an old antagonist of the A.F. of L.[35]

34. "Why the War Must Be Won" and "I Solemnly Promise," American Alliance publications, *ibid.*

35. For a short history of the Amalgamated, see Charles E. Zaretz, *The Amalgamated Clothing Workers of America* (New York, 1934); Mandel, *Samuel Gompers*, pp. 306-308; New York *Call*, Nov. 15, 19, 1917.

Nevertheless, the Alliance's decision to discredit these organizations if they failed to aid it in unifying labor on the East Side was a serious one. The Amalgamated had received war contracts for tents and uniforms, and the United Hebrew Trades was accepted by radical and conservative Jews alike as an agency essential to their ethnic labor movement.

Ignoring the danger of disrupting the needle trades by attacking the Amalgamated and its friends, Gompers ordered Ernest Bohm to act upon a resolution passed at the Buffalo convention calling on the Trades to co-operate with the A.F. of L. or face a pullout of the Federation's unions. Bohm carried the order to the offices of the Trades and left it with Pine. Word soon spread among the East Side labor leaders that Gompers intended to force the Trades to co-operate with the A.F. of L. whether it wished to or not. When Schlesinger of the International heard this news, he reacted quickly and promised Pine that his organization would not sit idly by and watch Gompers control the Jewish garment locals. It was not long before Gompers and Bohm realized that they would not easily force the Trades to co-operate.[36] Having second thoughts on the situation, Gompers asked Pine if it were not possible for the two of them to compromise their differences. Pine readily agreed to confer with Bohm at the Continental Hotel in New York.[37]

While Bohm and Pine prepared to meet, the Alliance became interested in a dispute between some unemployed ladies' garment workers and the Board of Labor Standards Control, which supervised working conditions in the East Side's defense plants. The board had been set up in August by Secretary of War Newton D. Baker to police the working conditions in the sweatshops.[38] Baker considered the board an important agency in keeping down disruptions in this vital area, and the board took on even more importance after Hillman had complained about the terrible working conditions in some of the shops fulfilling government contracts. The board was set up especially to prevent children under fifteen

36. New York *Call*, Nov. 24, 1917.
37. *Ibid.*, Dec. 12, 1917.
38. George Soule, *Sidney Hillman* (New York, 1939), p. 87; Matthew Josephson, *Sidney Hillman: Statesman of American Labor* (New York, 1952), p. 165.

years of age from working on government contracts, and to supervise collective bargaining procedures.[39]

In order to obtain a group of industrial relations experts knowledgeable enough to understand the various factions present in the garment industry, Baker had chosen Mrs. Florence Kelley, secretary of the National Consumers League, a lifetime crusader for improved working conditions; Louis E. Kirstein, the manager of Filene and Company of Boston; and Captain Walter Kreusi, of the Army Quartermaster Corps.[40] Whether Baker knew that Mrs. Kelley was a member of the Peoples Council and that Kirstein had socialist sympathies is uncertain. He may have chosen them to appease the liberals on the East Side; or his own sympathy for pacifism may have influenced his choice.[41]

Gompers' attention had been directed to the Board of Labor Standards Control when Maisel had informed him that the Amalgamated had refused to allow several thousand ladies' garment workers to share in government contracts awarded to Amalgamated-controlled industries. This practice amounted to enforcing a closed shop. Not knowing where else to turn, the unemployed garment workers had appealed to the Alliance for aid in finding employment. Since Maisel had believed that this situation might lead to the workers picketing the Amalgamated's shops and thus disrupting the garment industry, he had advised Gompers that the Alliance should take a hand in ending the dispute.[42]

Two months later Gompers received word from one of the A.F. of L.'s United Garment Workers unions that the Board of Labor Standards Control was again tolerating the Amalgamated's use of the closed shop at Cowen's Uniforms on Broadway. Because of this situation, Gompers was told, "Secretary Baker is forcing our people at Cowen to recognize the Amalgamated which is part of the Socialist Party and the Peoples Council."[43] Gompers was greatly upset because he had written Baker earlier that Cowen

39. Josephine Goldmark, *Impatient Crusader* (Urbana, Ill., 1953), pp. 128-130; Palmer, *Newton D. Baker*, I, 265.

40. Zaretz, *The Amalgamated*, pp. 116-117; Palmer, *Newton D. Baker*, I, 264.

41. C. H. Cramer, *Newton D. Baker: A Biography* (New York, 1961), p. 8.

42. Maisel to Gompers, Sept. 10, 1917, Gompers papers.

43. Larger to Gompers, telegram, Dec. 6, 1917, *ibid*.

wished to work with the loyal United Garment Workers Union, but was being pressured by the Amalgamated to sign a contract with its workers. The Board of Labor Standards Control, he told Baker, had refused to enter the dispute.[44]

Meanwhile, Gompers received word from Maisel that the increasing numbers of socialists and pacifists within the Amalgamated created an obstructionist threat which might prevent the union from fulfilling its defense contracts.[45] At the same time the *Jewish Morning Journal*, which was sympathetic to the Alliance, reported that the Amalgamated was responsible for the unemployed workers "starving for lack of work";[46] and Nathan Levine, a representative of the workers, had publicly begged for work in the A.F. of L.'s shops.[47]

Since Maisel was interested in gaining the loyalty of these people for the Alliance, he attended one of their meetings (at their request) and advised them to appeal to the International Garment Workers Union for aid.[48] The workers, however, knew that the International's president, Benjamin Schlesinger, was an ally of the Amalgamated, and they requested Maisel to help them find work.[49] Maisel told Gompers: "They assured me they are loyal, but have been misguided by the Amalgamated." He declared that the Alliance, in his opinion, should help the workers present their case to the government.[50] When Schlesinger learned that Maisel planned to assist the ladies' garment workers, he wired Gompers: "Pay no attention to the so-called unemployed garment workers. I have contacted the War Department to give them work."[51]

The workers did not depend on Schlesinger for aid. On December 18 a spokesman for the group wrote the Board of Labor Standards Control about their plight.[52] He declared in his letter that more than thirty thousand persons were unemployed as a

44. Gompers to Baker, Nov. 16, 1917, *ibid.*
45. Maisel to Gompers, telegram, Dec. 7, 1917, *ibid.*
46. *Jewish Morning Journal*, Dec. 7, 1917.
47. Nathan Levine to the *New Post*, Dec. 7, 1917, Gompers papers.
48. Maisel to Gompers, Dec. 10, 1917, *ibid.*
49. Maisel to Creel, Dec. 12, 1917, C.P.I. papers, 1-A1-26.
50. Maisel to Gompers, Dec. 12, 1917, Gompers papers.
51. Benjamin Schlesinger to Gompers, telegram, undated copy, *ibid.*
52. Charles Pajner to Gompers, Dec. 18, 1917, *ibid.*

result of the board's refusal to stop the Amalgamated from practicing the closed shop. The spokesman informed the board that his people had put their faith in the Alliance and the A.F. of L. as the most immediate way to find work.[53] Indeed Gompers had just given Maisel permission to bring the Alliance into the dispute and aid the workers in every way possible.[54]

Maisel hurriedly called a meeting of the unemployed workers at Webster Hall where he charged the Amalgamated with sowing dissension within the garment industry by its closed-shop practices. The situation was critical, Maisel asserted, because defense contracts were involved. He hinted that the fault lay with the Board of Labor Standards Control, which contained two prominent pacifist members. When Schlesinger and Schlossberg rose to defend the board, they were refused permission to speak; Schlesinger remarked to a New York *Call* reporter present that "a group of insidious people are trying to destroy the Amalgamated." Schlesinger interpreted the episode as an attempt to break the liberal labor movement on the East Side.[55]

By this time the situation had become so tense in the garment district that Creel feared a disruption of the industry. He ordered his aides to make a thorough investigation of all the issues involved. The report prepared for Creel declared that if the Board of Labor Standards Control tried to withhold contracts from the Amalgamated because it had excluded some laborers from its shops, there would be a complete breakdown of the garment industry. The Amalgamated believed, the report claimed, that Gompers was trying to force the government to award its contracts solely to the United Garment Workers unions. The report continued that on the other hand if the board did not support Gompers he "will be deprived of power and prestige." Creel's aides concluded that the entire quarrel was basically one between the A.F. of L. and the Amalgamated for control of the garment industry.[56] Since the situation was confused with charges of "obstructionism" on the one side and charges of "union rivalry" on the other, Creel refused to become involved. He decided to await the

53. Committee of Fifteen to L. K. Kirstein, report, Dec. 18, 1917, *ibid.*
54. Gompers to Maisel, Dec. 13, 1917, *ibid.*
55. New York *Call*, Dec. 16, 1917.
56. George Creel, confidential memorandum, Dec. 29, 1917, C.P.I. papers, 1-A1-26.

results of the investigation of the entire supply program by Senator Chamberlain's Committee.[57]

While the dispute concerning the Board of Labor Standards Control continued, Ernest Bohm and Max Pine began their discussions over the seating of the United Garment Workers in the United Hebrew Trades. Pine argued that if the United Garment Workers were seated, disputes would erupt between them and the Amalgamated's delegates, thus reducing the effectiveness of the Trades.[58] Nevertheless, Pine agreed to ask his organization to vote on admitting the A.F. of L.'s members. The following day, however, he requested more time to consider the situation; and two weeks later he delayed the vote until February when the Trade's general board could meet, as he asserted, "to fight it out."[59]

Pine's decision to delay action on Bohm's request was the result of a rumor that the War Department was preparing to reorganize its supply program.[60] The situation was uncertain and Pine chose to await the outcome of the investigations. The rumor proved correct. The entire supply system of the armed services was revamped, and in the process the Board of Labor Standards Control was abolished. But the circumstances surrounding the abolishing of the board greatly disturbed the socialists. For one thing, Mrs. Florence Kelley had resigned before the board was ordered out of existence.[61] The socialists claimed that she had been forced off the board because she was a pacifist. Moreover, they charged Secretary of War Baker with yielding to the demands of those who wished to drive all pacifists and socialists out of the government, the New York *Call* pointing out that Senator Wadsworth of New York had recently urged that no radicals be allowed to serve on government agencies.[62]

Shortly after the abolishing of the Board of Labor Standards Control, the general board of the United Hebrew Trades met after receiving a stern warning from Gompers that "all unions asso-

57. New York *Call*, Dec. 28, 1917.
58. *Ibid.*, Jan. 3, 1918.
59. *Ibid.*, Jan. 5, 17, 1918.
60. The *Call* (Jan. 27, 1918) reported that the War Department had been accused by the Senate of inefficiency in supplying the armed forces. See also New York *Times*, Jan. 26, 1918.
61. New York *Call*, Jan. 27, 1918.
62. *Ibid.*, Jan. 30, 1918; Zaretz, *The Amalgamated*, p. 118; Goldmark, *Impatient Crusader*, p. 131.

ciated with the A.F. of L. must be seated; all others unseated."[63] The meeting was attended by a mass of angry delegates as well as by an Alliance delegation led by Bohm and Maisel. The session went badly for the Alliance. Hardly had the question of seating the United Garment Workers been raised, when Schlesinger rose to demand that Gompers' people be excluded from the Trades. Bohm and Maisel attempted to speak but were shouted down by the delegates. They had to sit quietly while Schlesinger, Schlossberg, and Pine charged Gompers with trying to break the liberal labor movement in the garment industry. When a vote was taken on the question, only twenty-four out of one hundred delegates had voted for admission. Although there now was a possibility that Gompers might pull his unions from the Trades, the delegates were willing to take the chance. As one expressed it, "Perhaps now the United Hebrew Trades will have more energy."[64]

The Trades' refusal to admit the United Garment Workers, and the Board of Labor Standards Control's earlier refusal to interfere with the Amalgamated's use of the closed shop, were not total defeats for the Alliance. The A.F. of L. continued to apply pressure on the Trades by threatening to pull its unions out of that organization. This threat, combined with the breakdown of the pacifist position in the spring of 1918, led the radicals to tone down their agitation. On March 8 Maisel informed Gompers that the Trades was to "discuss a possible change in its attitude"; because of this the East Side was quiet.[65]

The background to Gompers' success in getting the government to supervise more closely the Amalgamated's use of the closed shop is less clear. Although the Board of Labor Standards Control containing Mrs. Kelley and Kirstein was abolished during the reorganization of the War Department, Gompers' role here is uncertain. It appears that the board was abolished during the over-all reorganizational process and not as an attempt to placate Gompers. In fact, Kirstein remained in the supply program, much to the A.F. of L.'s disapproval.[66]

63. Gompers to A.F. of L. Executive Committee, Jan. 29, 1918; Gompers to United Hebrew Trades, Jan. 25, 1918, Gompers papers.
64. New York *Call*, Feb. 6, 1918; Maisel to Gompers, Feb. 9, 1918, Gompers papers.
65. Maisel to Gompers, March 8, 1918, Gompers papers.
66. Larger to Gompers, Feb. 4, 1918, *ibid.*

Gompers' quarrels with the liberal labor movement in New York City produced a severe crisis within the Alliance. Whereas the A.F. of L. faction backed their chief's actions in attacking the Trades and challenging the Amalgamated, the pro-war socialist faction was suspicious of Gompers' motives. He looked too much like a labor tsar bent on breaking his rivals. Gompers' real motivation may never be known; but his decision to bring the Alliance into a dispute which had all the characteristics of an inter-union squabble, made the organization appear simply a pawn in labor's wars. By February, 1918, there was the threat of a serious schism in the Alliance. Fearing that the Alliance would break up, Maisel appealed to Creel "to aid in preventing a split between our radicals and labormen."[67] There is no evidence showing that Creel came to the aid of Maisel, but the Alliance did not topple. Wilson's Fourteen Points had captured the imagination of the pro-war socialists and rekindled their faith in the loyalty issue.

Chapter 7. The Fourteen Points and Labor Diplomacy

President Wilson's presentation of the Fourteen Points to the Senate on January 8, 1918, came at a low point in the Alliance program to "Americanize" the anti-war labor unions. The agency's reputation as a non-partisan organization had suffered after the A.F. of L. had attacked the Amalgamated and the United Hebrew Trades. The Alliance's effort to unify labor in New York City was seriously curtailed, and the old charges that America was fighting a "capitalistic war" continued to come forth from the radical unions. These anti-war forces had taken advantage of Wilson's vagueness on American war aims to insist that he spoke, not for the American people, but for a select group of industrial barons who would profit from the war. The crux of the matter was the President's long delay in declaring America's precise war objectives. Actually not all anti-war radicals deliberately misrepresented Wilson's position; some of them simply were confused as to what that position was. As the President failed to make a clear declaration of America's war aims, the Alliance leadership was

67. Maisel to Creel, Feb. 28, 1918, *ibid.*

forced to fall back on the same old pro-war arguments to defend the Administration's policies.

The situation worsened perceptibly when the Bolsheviks overturned the Kerenski government and officially committed Russia to a peace based on no indemnities, no annexations, and the self-determination of all people. These Bolshevik proposals had appealed to many workers as the only way to obtain a quick negotiated peace, and Wilson had been thrown on the defensive by the Bolshevik solution to the war because he had had nothing better to offer the world as an alternative.

Realizing that America needed something immediately to stop the pacifist agitation at home as well as to counter the Bolshevik peace propaganda abroad, Wilson formulated a war aims program which he hoped would swing the initiative for peace back to the Allies. On January 8 the President announced his Fourteen Points program for peace.[1] One point, the fourteenth, called for an association of nations to guarantee world tranquillity, and clearly incorporated an idea similar to the one advocated by the Bolsheviks. The remaining points, too, contained much that was similar to the Russian program: the self-determination of all peoples, and the idea of no indemnities. Wilson's Fourteen Points were a worthy contribution toward ending the war and were soon being seriously discussed by friend and foe alike.

Earlier, the State Department, in conjunction with the C.P.I., had been working to wean the Russian people from the Bolsheviks in favor of the Allies.[2] Gompers' co-operation in assuring the Russian worker that American labor supported the Wilson Administration's policies was an important part of this program. Gompers subsequently was asked to supply the C.P.I. with every loyalty statement released by the Alliance as well as the A.F. of L. in support of the war effort.[3] At the same time, Creel cautioned the Alliance not to be too harsh on the Bolsheviks until the situation became clearer as to whether Russia could be kept in the war.[4]

1. Leonard, ed., *War Addresses of Woodrow Wilson*, "Address to Congress," Jan. 8, 1918, pp. 92-101.
2. Creel to Maisel, Jan. 4, 1918, C.P.I. papers, 1-A1-26. Creel advised Maisel that "Our representative in Petrograd is making good friendships."
3. Creel to Gompers, Jan. 29, 1918, *ibid.*
4. Creel to Maisel, Feb. 8, 1918, *ibid.* Creel advised, "Go easy on the Bolsheviki. I do not want them attacked, neither do I want them upheld."

With this task in mind, Gompers announced plans for a series of rallies starting February 7 in support of the Fourteen Points and labor loyalty. He called this period "labor's loyalty week" and emphasized that it was to demonstrate labor's "faith in democracy" by opposing those in America who would call for another international peace conference to stop the war.[5] For this task, the Alliance was offered the support of the National Security League, the National Civic Federation, the American Defense Society, and the Labor Loyalty League in an unprecedented display of domestic solidarity.[6] Gompers, for his part, took advantage of the series to publicize labor's loyalty by dispatching copies of the week's programs to every member of Congress; while Maisel asked that Secretary of War Baker and Secretary of Labor William B. Wilson address several of the week's rallies in order to demonstrate the Administration's support of labor.[7]

While numerous Alliance rallies took place in every major city, the most impressive one occurred on the night of February 10 in the Century Theatre in New York. The theater was brightly decked with red, white, and blue drapes, as well as the flags of the Allied nations. On the stage sat Secretary of Labor Wilson, Rabbi Stephen S. Wise, Hugh Frayne and James Duncan of the A.F. of L., and Maisel of the Alliance. The rally was especially significant because, for the first time since the Buffalo convention in November, 1917, a member of the Administration appeared to address a labor function.[8]

For three hours representatives of the Alliance, America's "loyal" Jews, the pro-war socialists, and the Administration outdid themselves in pledging their co-operation to the war effort. Frayne and Duncan promised that the A.F. of L. would never obstruct the war, and Secretary Wilson in turn pledged that his department had every intention of co-operating with the A.F. of L.'s wartime programs. Rabbi Wise, for his part, pledged the continued co-operation of America's pro-war Jews to the Administration and read a similar message from John Spargo represent-

5. New York *Times*, Jan. 7, 1918; Gompers, *Seventy Years*, II, 382.
6. Francis Preston to Gompers, Jan. 10, 1918, Gompers papers; New York *Times*, Feb. 6, 1918.
7. Gompers to Maisel, Jan. 16, 1918; Maisel to Gompers, Feb. 1, 1918, Gompers papers.
8. New York *Times*, Feb. 10, 1918.

ing the pro-war socialists. Wise also read a statement from Secretary of War Baker, who was unable to attend the rally. Baker expressed his confidence that the War Department would do all that it could to see that wholesome working conditions existed in the nation's war plants. He, too, pledged the fullest co-operation with the A.F. of L. in maintaining labor peace at home. The rally adjourned with the speakers standing before the audience holding hands in a gesture of unity.[9] A New York *Times* reporter present jubilantly declared, "The war has worked wonders in unifying labor"; while Maisel enthusiastically wrote Gompers, who was absent, that the rally was a complete success.[10]

Another rally was held twelve days later at the Lexington Theatre on February 22, Washington's birthday. Once again the Administration co-operated as Secretary of the Navy Josephus Daniels became the second member of the Cabinet in two weeks to address a labor function.[11] The theater again was decorated with red, white, and blue drapes as Louise Homer, who had sung for the Alliance in Grand Central Station, appeared at the request of Gompers.[12] Shortly thereafter Daniels rose to speak.

He addressed the gathering in a "Wilsonian" manner as he praised labor for helping make the world safe for democracy by supporting the war effort. In return for this co-operation, he predicted, the A.F. of L. would never again have to return to those prewar days which favored capital over labor.[13] Daniels' optimism was echoed by Gompers, who declared that after the war labor would be respected by the government because it had proved that the workingman could act responsibly in the national interest. Pacing up and down the stage, Gompers appealed to those assembled to continue to support the Administration's war program. He dramatically pointed his finger at the audience and shouted for them "to stand united and make every sacrifice for freedom." He urged the audience to go out and work for labor peace, to put down dissension, to oppose every form of radicalism, and to back

9. *Ibid.*, Feb. 11, 1918.
10. Maisel to Gompers, telegram, Feb. 11, 1917, Gompers papers.
11. Gompers to Secretary of the Navy Daniels, Feb. 14, 1918, *ibid.* New York *Times*, Feb. 23, 1918.
12. Gompers to all Alliance unions, Feb. 23, 1918, Gompers papers.
13. New York *Times*, Feb. 23, 1918.

up the men on the front lines.[14] His appeal for continued support of the Wilson Administration did not go unheeded, for it had been apparent since the Buffalo convention that the President was prepared to co-operate with conservative labor. The support of the Secretaries of War, Labor, and the Navy demonstrated further the Administration's determination to use the Alliance to hold labor behind the war effort.

After these loyalty rallies, the Alliance pushed its organizational campaigns until 136 locals existed in thirty-nine states, and 150 newspapers were publishing Alliance propaganda. Maisel confidently reported "that all of the nation's leading Jewish papers are now cooperating except the socialist ones." At this point, the Alliance had distributed one million pamphlets throughout the country and had held more than two hundred rallies.[15] Reports from the East Side were equally optimistic as pacifist agitation there dropped to a new low. Gompers was so pleased with the progress of the Alliance, he boasted that labor radicalism soon would come to an end.[16]

But the picture was not that bright. Rose Pastor Stokes suddenly resigned from the Alliance and prophetically declared that Gompers' plan of uniting labor and capital under the jurisdiction of the federal government was unrealistic. Mrs. Stokes switched to the Council and began speaking against Gompers and the Administration. During these weeks, too, there were the usual rumblings from Spargo's faction that Gompers was trying to stifle socialist autonomy within the Alliance.[17]

As the Alliance continued to support the government, Maisel called upon Creel to finance an ever-expanding loyalty program. Misunderstandings immediately resulted from Maisel's requests for more funds. The C.P.I. had just survived an intensive investigation by the Senate, and Creel was not anxious to increase his

14. Gompers, speech, Lexington Theatre, Feb. 22, 1918, copy, C.P.I. papers, A1-1.
15. American Alliance report, Feb. 20, 1918, Gompers papers.
16. Maisel to Gompers, Feb. 20, 1918; Gompers to New York *Tribune*, March 7, 1918, *ibid.*
17. Rose Pastor Stokes to Chester Wright, Feb. 25, 1918, *ibid.*; Maisel to Creel, Feb. 28, 1918, C.P.I. papers, 1-A5. Rose Pastor Stokes had hardly left the Alliance when she was arrested for spreading sedition. Later she was fined for applauding in the courtroom during the Debs sedition trial. See New York *Call*, May 31, June 4, Aug. 2, Sept. 11, 1918.

outlays at this time. He fully realized the value of keeping his books balanced until Congress turned its attention to more pressing matters. Consequently he refused to finance Maisel's budget requests because he considered them excessive at a time when disloyalty appeared to be on the decline.[18] The loyal Jewish Socialists League, however, disagreed with Creel and feared a resurgence of pacifism in the needle trades unless another series of rallies was carried out on the East Side. Nevertheless, Maisel could do nothing as Creel refused to finance any further programs at this time.[19]

With Creel curtailing expenses, Maisel had no other choice but to try to raise funds on his own. Gompers tried to aid the director by asking his friends for donations to the Alliance. The results were disappointing. Maisel then made several eastern and midwestern appearances among the A.F. of L.'s unions, but these organizations were not affluent enough to contribute sufficiently to the Alliance. In desperation, Maisel returned to Creel for support; but as before Creel refused to co-operate, fearing the Senate more than Maisel. He declined to finance anything other than the usual publications, salaries, and rentals.[20]

By this time Creel had tired of Maisel's constant pleas for money and he complained bitterly to Gompers about the situation. Creel's complaints worried Gompers that Maisel might upset the delicate relationship between the C.P.I. and the Alliance, and he ordered Maisel to stop bothering Creel with his problems.[21] The peppery director was not one to mince words, however, and he retorted that Creel did not want to approve any of the Alliance's new programs unless they involved loyalty work within the immediate New York area.[22]

In the meantime, Creel's orders to cut back on the Alliance's expenditures had gone through the C.P.I.'s accounting offices, and many bills were returned to Maisel unpaid.[23] Not knowing where

18. Creel to Maisel, March 1, 1918; Byoir to Maisel, March 6, 1918, C.P.I. papers, 1-A6.
19. Maisel to Byoir, March 6, 1918, *ibid.*
20. Maisel to Gompers, March 22, 1918, *ibid.*, 1-A5; Byoir to Maisel, March 13, 1918, *ibid.*, 1-A6.
21. Gompers to Maisel, March 14, 1918, Gompers papers.
22. Maisel to Gompers, March 15, 1918, *ibid.*
23. Creel to Byoir, March 14, 1918, C.P.I. papers, 1-A1; Maisel to Lee, March 18, 1918, *ibid.*, 1-A5.

to get additional funds to meet these unexpected expenses, Maisel again appealed to Gompers for help. The president of the A.F. of L. did not intend to solve all of the Alliance's problems himself, and he curtly advised Maisel to pay his own bills.[24] On March 19, Maisel hurriedly attempted to arrange a new rapport with Creel: "If my efforts have not fully come up to your expectations it may be that there are obstacles which you do not appreciate."[25] Creel would not relent, though, and once again, Maisel desperately appealed to Gompers for aid.[26] By this time Gompers was clearly upset with Maisel's pleas and he ordered the director to either use labor's own funds to finance the Alliance or cut back his programs. Upon receiving this order from Gompers, Maisel glumly wrote Stokes that the Alliance's treasury would soon be depleted if funds were not quickly forthcoming.[27]

Gompers' failure to aid the Alliance at this time was not because of disinterestedness on his part, but because of his heavy commitments to the A.F. of L.'s wartime programs and his involvement in aiding the Administration to "sell" its Fourteen Points abroad. Gompers' interest in the international scene had been lifelong. After years of corresponding with labor leaders in Europe, Asia, and South America, he had become known abroad as America's most powerful labor tsar and the unchallenged leader of conservative labor in America. Some world socialist leaders severely criticized Gompers for not pushing a more radical labor reform program at home, but the Administration did not fail to use Gompers' reputation among conservative labor leaders abroad to support America's war aims. As early as September, 1917, Gompers and the State Department had discussed sending to Russia a delegation of A.F. of L. and pro-war socialists to demonstrate American support for the Kerenski government.[28] Likewise,

24. Gompers to Maisel, March 18, 1918, *ibid.*, 1-A5.
25. Maisel to Creel, March 19, 1918, *ibid.*
26. Maisel to Gompers, March 21, 1918, *ibid.*
27. Gompers to Maisel, March 22, 1918, Gompers papers; Maisel to Stokes, March 28, 1918, Stokes papers, Box 30.
28. Gompers, *Seventy Years*, II, 398; New York *Times*, Sept. 15, 1917. Spargo related that Wilson offered to pay part of this mission's expenses from his own National Defense Fund, but Spargo insisted that the entire mission be a voluntary one (Spargo to Gompers, Sept. 20, 1917, Stokes papers, Box 28).

Gompers had sent to Ambassador Francis a message for the work-ingmen's councils of Russia expressing the A.F. of L.'s solid endorsement of Wilson's total victory concept.[29]

Throughout 1917 Gompers had conducted a continuous cor-respondence with his colleagues in the Allied countries, and espe-cially those in Great Britain. By January, 1918, just prior to Wilson's release of the Fourteen Points, Gompers and the C.P.I. had worked out plans to invite to the United States a mission headed by W. A. Appleton of the British Federation of Labor to witness the A.F. of L.'s determination in support of the war effort.[30] The State Department hurriedly approved these plans, and Wilson himself ordered Creel to do all that was necessary to assist the project.[31]

Gompers' co-operation with the war effort had become in-creasingly important to Washington, for ominous rumors had begun to filter back from Europe that Allied labor was tiring of the war and might yield to the Bolshevik pleas for a ceasefire.[32] Gompers and Creel made plans in March to send to Europe an A.F. of L. mission, headed by John Frey and seven others, in-cluding Chester Wright of the Alliance. Wright was ordered to send back news articles about the determination of Allied labor to remain in the war.[33] Moreover, the Alliance was given the task of seeing that the British mission to the United States was properly impressed with the A.F. of L.'s support of the war effort. To ensure that the British got a flattering picture of American labor, Gompers ordered James Roche and Collis Lovely of the A.F. of L. to accompany the mission around the country.[34] For his part, Gompers spoke in glowing terms of the Federation's

29. Wilson, memorandum, Sept. 18, 1917, Wilson papers; New York *Times*, Sept. 19, 1917; Chester Wright to Gompers, Sept. 28, 1917, Gom-pers papers.
30. New York *Times*, Jan. 5, 1918; Gompers, *Seventy Years*, II, 384.
31. Lombardi, *Labor's Voice*, p. 207; Wilson to Creel, Jan. 9, 1918, C.P.I. papers, 1-A1.
32. Gompers to Wilson, Jan. 17, 1918; Wilson to Gompers, Jan. 19, 1918, Wilson papers.
33. Gompers to Wright, Jan. 29, 1918, Gompers papers; Gompers to John Frey, Feb. 15, 1918, John Frey papers, Library of Congress.
34. Executive meeting report, American Alliance, Feb. 21, 1918, Gom-pers papers.

importance to the government in keeping down labor radicalism at home.[35] Prior to the mission's departure for home, he asked Creel to give the delegates copies of the Alliance pamphlet, "The Battle Line of Democracy," to distribute "to some friend in England, it might be helpful."[36]

While Gompers was involved in seeing that the British got the best possible picture of the A.F. of L., Creel asked him confidentially to accompany the A.F. of L.'s mission to Europe. Realizing that he might not have given Gompers enough time to consider the matter, Creel nevertheless made it clear that the Administration had decided that it was of the utmost importance for Gompers to go abroad and uphold the President's policies before the Allies.[37]

The Administration's urgency to send Gompers overseas was intensified when word reached Washington that the Bolsheviks had signed a separate peace treaty (Brest-Litovsk) with Germany. The situation was critical; the Russians were not only withdrawing from the war, but Allied labor after living for years under the most adverse wartime conditions was becoming restive for peace. Gompers glumly informed Maisel of the seriousness of the situation and, consequently, of the increased importance of the A.F. of L.'s mission abroad.[38]

At this point news reached Washington that Arthur Henderson, the leader of a pacifist labor faction in Britain, was planning to bring a mission to the United States and explain their point of view to the American worker. Henderson had been forced out of the government in August, 1917, for his support of the Stockholm peace movement and was a well-known agitator for immediate peace.[39] As late as February, 1918, he had urged Gompers to send representatives to an inter-Allied conference in London to discuss a negotiated peace. Fortunately for Gompers the invita-

35. Gompers, press release, Feb. 21, 1918, copy in *ibid.*
36. Gompers to Creel, March 23, 1918, C.P.I. papers, 1-A1-17.
37. Creel to Gompers, Feb. 14, 1918, *ibid.* Creel concluded, "I do believe that it is of the utmost importance for you to go abroad very soon. Will you think it over?"
38. Gompers to Maisel, March 26, 1918, *ibid.*; James Bunyan and H. H. Fisher, *The Bolsheviki Revolution* (Stanford, 1934), p. 538.
39. Gankin and Fisher, *The Bolsheviks and the World War*, pp. 601-602.

tion had arrived too late and the A.F. of L. could do nothing about the matter.[40]

When Henderson's plans became known in Washington, Wilson was disturbed that this mission might ignite another outburst of pacifism. The President remarked that should Henderson's group be allowed into the country the situation would "be fraught with the greatest mischief."[41] This frank disapproval by the President, combined with the British government's reluctance to allow a pacifist mission outside the United Kingdom, forced Henderson to cancel his plans. When Chester Wright, then preparing to leave for Europe with the A.F. of L. mission, heard the news, he exclaimed with relief, "We don't have to worry about keeping them out now!"[42]

Everything was ready for the A.F. of L. mission to leave from New York via military convoy for Europe. The delegates sailed on March 29 with all the enthusiasm of those embarking on a cause vital to the world labor movement. But once at sea, their enthusiasm waned when they were subjected to the military discipline of convoy life. Although they were ordered to remain below deck at night, these precautions failed to prevent a German U-boat from firing a torpedo which missed their ship by only eight feet and struck an accompanying cruiser.[43]

Escaping the hazards of the sea, the mission landed in England only to witness that same night a German zeppelin raid on British coastal shipping. Not until the delegates reached London did they relax and enjoy the hospitality of George Barnes, conservative leader of British labor. They were not in England to relax, though. Soon the group was addressing hundreds of workers, many of them socialists and pacifists who had been severely critical of the Wilson Administration's policies.[44] As the mission traveled throughout Britain, Chester Wright prepared propaganda articles for home consumption. Basically, Wright told Americans that

40. Gompers, *Seventy Years*, II, 396, 403; Gompers to Arthur Henderson, telegram, Feb. 18, 1918, Gompers papers.
41. Baker, *Woodrow Wilson: Life and Letters*, VIII, 44-45. Henderson eventually toured Canada (New York *Call*, May 8, 1918).
42. Wright to Gompers, March 27, 1918, Gompers papers.
43. Wright to Creel, March 28, 1918, C.P.I. papers, 1-A1-5.
44. *Proceedings*, 38th annual A.F. of L. convention, St. Paul, June 10-20, 1918, "Report of the Labor Mission," pp. 138-151.

British labor was not tiring of the war, would not give in to the peace propaganda coming from Russia, and could be counted upon to stand with the Wilson Administration until Germany surrendered.[45]

Having completed their tour of Britain, the members of the mission crossed the channel to France where they traveled to Paris. There they spoke with representatives of French, Greek, and Serbian labor.[46] As in England the mission delegates stood firmly for the Fourteen Points and made it especially clear to France's large socialist party that the A.F. of L. would not support a Stockholm peace conference nor agree to the Bolshevik peace proposals. They urged, instead, that the French socialists accept Wilson's Fourteen Points as a reasonable way to end the war. The mission then left for a tour of the battlefronts.[47]

While the A.F. of L. representatives toured Europe, the Alliance and the C.P.I. prepared to capitalize on the propaganda value of the trip by planning a gala reception for the returning mission at the A.F. of L.'s thirty-eighth annual convention in St. Paul, Minnesota. The Alliance was given the job of arranging the reception, and Maisel with his pockets full of C.P.I. money departed for St. Paul on June 3. Among his possessions was a telegram from President Wilson expressing his satisfaction with the A.F. of L.'s "labor ambassadors" abroad.[48] When the mission returned from Europe in late May, the delegates were transported hurriedly to St. Paul where they were greeted at an Alliance-sponsored reception by Gompers and a large contingent of St. Paul businessmen. The mission was wined and dined in an atmosphere of labor-management good will. Maisel was certain that the reception would do much to cement better labor relations in the Midwest.[49]

45. Chester Wright, "England in Wartime," a series of Alliance releases published in the nation's press, copies in Gompers papers.

46. Maisel to Gompers, April 29, 1918, Gompers papers.

47. New York *Times*, May 8, 1918; also *Proceedings*, A.F. of L. convention, "Report of the Labor Mission," pp. 140-151.

48. Maisel to Byoir, June 3, 1918; Maisel to Byoir, June 11, 1918, C.P.I. papers, 1-A6.

49. Mock and Larson, *Words That Won the War*, p. 206; John Frey, speech, St. Paul, undated copy, Gompers papers; Maisel, report, St. Paul convention and reception, June 5-22, 1918, *ibid*. On June 2, 1918, the New York *Call* printed an editorial, "Our Labor Mission Returns," which

A spirit of good will continued to be manifest in the convention when Julius Schmahl, secretary of the state of Minnesota, loudly praised the A.F. of L. for its loyal stand with the Wilson Administration. When it was Gompers' turn to speak, he lived up to his image by attacking the socialists for "obstructionism" and "outliving their usefulness." But the old chief had a surprise in store for his delegates. He dramatically announced that he had wanted to travel to Europe and talk with the Allied labor leaders there. Now the opportunity had presented itself, he said: another Inter-Allied Trade Union Conference had been scheduled for London in September and he believed it important that he represent the A.F. of L. With a minimum of dissent the convention authorized Gompers to attend the conference.[50]

As the St. Paul convention progressed, Maisel took the opportunity to address several Alliance locals in Duluth and St. Paul, attempting to impress upon them the need for continued loyalty work in the Midwest. Yet he heard only good news from these chapters. Mayor Thomas Van Lear had resigned from the council movement, and consequently the pacifists' program in that area had been thrown into complete confusion. Maisel became so enthusiastic over this news that he recklessly exclaimed, "These cities will yield a one hundred per cent loyalty as a result of our meetings here!"[51]

There is little question that the Alliance's reception for the A.F. of L. mission and Gompers' loyal statements at St. Paul did much to improve the Federation's image as a responsible labor organization. At the same time the Alliance and the C.P.I. had successfully used the mission to keep the American worker informed on the determination of his European counterpart to see

---

emphasized that the A.F. of L. mission did not represent the country's socialist elements. On June 18 the *Call* reported that the mission was greeted with "the sounds of tinkling cymbals."

50. For the complete proceedings of the reception and convention, see *Proceedings*, 38th A.F. of L. convention, St. Paul, pp. 1-134. Also see Gompers, *Seventy Years*, II, 409. On June 11, 1918, the New York *Call* labeled Gompers' plans to tour Europe "an unholy alliance between Gompers and capital." On June 18 the *Call* declared that Gompers' mission was to rid Europe of socialism.

51. Maisel, report, St. Paul, June 5-22, 1918, C.P.I. papers, 1-A5; New York *Call*, June 18, 1918. Van Lear had cooled his pacifist sympathies because he was preparing to run in a non-partisan primary for mayor.

the war through to a victorious conclusion. This did much to convince the A.F. of L.'s rank-and-file that the Allied worker would not support the Bolshevik peace proposals or another international peace conference at Stockholm. If the A.F. of L. mission accomplished nothing else, it helped to bring Allied and American labor closer together at a time when the war was reaching a critical stage.[52]

In the meantime an Allied and Neutral Socialist Conference had been called for London in June by the pacifist Arthur Henderson. The conference was to discuss ways to bring about peace through the good offices of the neutral socialists who had contacts on both sides of the battlefields. The Wilson Administration was anxious that representatives of the pro-war socialist faction be present to declare their support for America's war program. Creel was given the job of choosing these representatives, and he asked Spargo, A. M. Simons, Alexander Howatt of the United Mine Workers in Kansas, Louis Kopelin, editor of the *New Appeal* in Kansas, and Charles E. Russell, who was in London working for the C.P.I., to compose the mission. These socialists readily agreed to support the Administration.[53]

After the dangerous Atlantic crossing, the pro-war socialists traveled to London where they began a busy schedule of speaking at luncheons, banquets, and numerous anti-war rallies in Trafalgar Square. When the sessions of the Allied and Neutral Socialist Conference opened, Spargo's people spoke eloquently for Wilson's Fourteen Points. At the same time they made it clear that America's pro-war socialists did not support the Bolshevik peace demands. Although they were in the minority, the group did much to prevent the anti-war socialists from taking any concrete efforts to set up another international peace conference. Back home the Alliance publicized throughout the labor movement the mission's strong stand for the Wilson Administration. The Socialist party,

52. Chester Wright's "Save Space in Ships for United States Soldiers" and "Allied Labor Alignment Never So Solid as Now" were distributed in the United States and throughout Great Britain.
53. For an excessively detailed account of the pro-war socialist mission to Europe, see Miriam Simons Leuck, "The American Socialist and Labor Mission to Europe, 1918: Background, Activities, and Significance, An Experiment in Diplomatic Diplomacy," unpublished Ph.D. dissertation, Northwestern University, 1941.

however, did not take this propaganda lightly. It publicly announced that although a small number of former socialists were in London attending the conference, the party which represented the majority of American socialists had not been allowed delegates by the Wilson Administration.[54]

Throughout the spring of 1918, while the A.F. of L. and Alliance co-operated with the government in sending "labor ambassadors" abroad, the Peoples Council attempted to make its voice heard in international affairs. Wilson's issuance of the Fourteen Points pleasantly surprised the radicals and rekindled their faith in the Administration. Many of these people were impressed by the similarity of Wilson's program with that of the Bolsheviks. Then, too, some of them believed that if Wilson were willing to declare a war aims program which seemed to embody some socialist proposals, the President might have become open-minded toward a negotiated peace. This enthusiasm for the Fourteen Points is clearly illustrated. On January 5 before the program had been announced, Hillquit and Nearing once again had called upon Wilson to accept the Bolshevik proposals as the only just way to end the war. Again on January 7 the Socialist party declared that the Bolshevik plan held the only hope of securing a lasting peace.[55] Yet shortly after the President released the Fourteen Points, many socialists were acclaiming Wilson's demands as if they had been their own. One day later a personage as important as Morris Hillquit happily interpreted Wilson's program as agreeing with the "main principles" of that laid down by the Bolsheviks.[56] Nearing, however, was not as optimistic and urged his followers to continue their agitation for the Russian proposals.[57] On the other hand, Max Eastman was favorably impressed with Wilson's program, and Meyer London, the only socialist member of the House of Representatives, spoke highly of the plan in Congress.[58] Elizabeth

54. New York *Times*, June 24, 1918; Paul Kellogg and Arthur Gleason, *British Labor and the War* (London, 1919), p. 308; New York *Call*, June 21, 1918.

55. New York *Call*, Jan. 6, 8, 1918.

56. *Ibid.*, Jan. 9, 1918.

57. Scott Nearing, "Democracy and Peace," P.C.A. publication, Jan. 10, 1918, Tamiment Institute; New York *Call*, Jan. 15, 1918.

58. Bell, "Background and Development," p. 316; *Congressional Record*, House of Representatives, 65th Congress, second session, Jan. 11, 1918, pp. 861-862.

Freeman, convinced that the President had accepted the Russian proposals in principle, urged her co-workers to work even harder for peace because "Trotsky, Lenin, Lloyd George and President Wilson are on our side and the People are ready to listen to us!"[59] Believing that the President had softened his stand on the war, the Socialist party decided to send delegates to the Inter-Allied Socialist Conference in London;[60] earlier the party had had trouble sending a cablegram out of the country.[61] Moreover, Henderson had extended an invitation to the A.F. of L.'s socialists because anti-Administration socialists were not allowed to leave the country.[62] Despite these handicaps, the party prepared to hold a conference of all socialist, labor, and radical groups to draw up a war aims program and elect a delegate to carry it to London.[63] Council officials aided in the project, and Lochner had appealed to Jane Addams to be that delegate. The shy Miss Addams refused to become involved. Although disappointed, Lochner had kept her informed of the proceedings.[64] Preparations for the conference continued unabated, and the socialists dispatched a cablegram to the Bolsheviks declaring that they hoped to be represented at the London conference.[65]

Feeling that the time was right to compromise the differences between the Wilsonian and Bolshevik peace plans, the party opened its conference in Bryan Hall on February 16, at the same time the Alliance was holding its "labor loyalty week." Approximately three hundred delegates heard Nearing, Hillquit, and Rabbi Judah L. Magnes call for a compromise war aims program which would be advantageous to the world's working classes. The delegates, who represented numerous peace societies in the area, worked for two days on a program incorporating the Bolshevik proposals as well as Wilson's "freedom of the seas" and international peace-keeping machinery.[66] After the program had been

59. Elizabeth Freeman to co-workers, Jan. 15, 1918, Swarthmore.
60. Kellogg and Gleason, *British Labor and the War*, pp. 268-269.
61. New York *Call*, Jan. 27, 1918; Executive Council minutes, P.C.A., Jan. 26, 1918, Swarthmore.
62. P.C.A. *Bulletin*, Vol. I, No. 14, Feb. 14, 1918, Tamiment Institute.
63. New York *Call*, Feb. 10, 1918.
64. Lochner to Addams, Feb. 2, 1918, Woman's Peace Party papers, Swarthmore.
65. New York *Call*, Feb. 12, 14, 1918.
66. P.C.A. press release, Feb. 16, 1918, Swarthmore; New York *Times*,

completed, a vote was taken to determine who should carry the plan to London. On February 17 the delegates reassembled in the Central Opera House to hear James Maurer proclaimed as that delegate; Elizabeth Freeman declared that more than $4,000 had been pledged toward Maurer's expenses.[67] Shortly thereafter, Hillquit read the program to an enthusiastic socialist rally in Carnegie Hall. When Gompers was informed of the socialists' plans, he publicly announced that the London meeting was nothing more than an attempt by Europe's socialists to gain a "pro-German peace."[68]

Despite Gompers' harsh words, Maurer optimistically applied to the State Department for a passport to Great Britain. But the day of judgment was at hand. The socialists awakened from their dreams of Wilsonian benevolence when the State Department flatly rejected Maurer's application. Maurer was informed that "only special war cases" were allowed to travel through the war zones. The New York *Call* protested vigorously in an editorial, "Strangled Again," and the Council, fully aware that the A.F. of L. had just dispatched its own missions to Europe, complained bitterly that they could not understand the government's "reasons in keeping one socialist representative at home."[69]

The radicals were jolted further by the Administration when Scott Nearing and the Socialist Society of New York were indicted for distributing "The Great Madness," which summed up Nearing's grievances against the Wilson Administration.[70] Council pacifists immediately started raising money to defend their director from an "attack upon the right of dissent, which if not put down, would bear upon the future of freedom in the United

Feb. 17, 18, 1918; New York *Call*, Feb. 17, 18, 1918; "Resolutions of the National Conference of Labor, Socialists, and Radical Movements," Feb. 16-17, 1918, copy in Woman's Peace Party papers, Swarthmore.

67. New York *Times*, Feb. 18, 1918; New York *Call*, Feb. 19, 1918; P.C.A. *Bulletin*, Vol. I, No. 16, March 1, 1918, Tamiment Institute.

68. Hillquit, speech, Carnegie Hall, Feb. 20, 1918, Swarthmore; New York *Call*, Feb. 22, 1918. Henderson called on Gompers to take back his statements about the London conference being in "favor of a German peace" (*ibid.*, March 1, 1918).

69. P.C.A. *Bulletin*, Vol. I, No. 20, May 1, 1918, Tamiment Institute; New York *Call*, March 4, 1918.

70. New York *Call*, March 23, 1918; "The Great Madness," pamphlet, copy in Debs file, Tamiment Institute.

States." Nearing's trial dragged out for several months, but he won the decision. The Socialist Society, however, which had printed the pamphlet, was fined $3,000 for spreading seditious material through the mails.[71]

When the radicals realized that Wilson's Fourteen Points did not necessarily indicate a change in the President's attitude toward a negotiated peace, they once again agitated for a quick end to the war. Starting on May Day, the Council, in co-operation with the Socialist party, sponsored a series of rallies in support of the German socialists, whom the Council contended were anxious to see peace restored as soon as possible. Sidney Hillman, Schlossberg, and Panken addressed a large peace rally in Madison Square Garden on the virtues of international socialism.[72] Panken spoke again on the East Side at the Grand Theatre, where Schlossberg openly praised Karl Marx for his "realistic program outlining the true goals of the working classes." Another rally was held at the Central Opera House, where Senator William Mason of Illinois attacked universal military training (which was being debated in Congress) as a part of the Administration's desire to "prussianize" the American people. Mason was followed by Isaac Bainbridge, editor of the Canadian *Forward*, who spoke of the socialists' right to share in the making of a final peace treaty. The rally closed with Norman Thomas and Rabbi Magnes outlining new ways to correspond with the socialists of other nations.[73]

Several days later the Council called a three-day conference of all labor, socialist, and radical groups at the Peoples House, New York City, to seek ways to co-operate with pacifist groups in Europe. Nearing opened the conference by declaring that the anti-war forces within the United States had been prevented by the Wilson Administration from communicating with the "democratic movements" in other countries. Nearing readily admitted that the President had succeeded in isolating the Socialist party and its allies from their friends overseas. The meeting concluded on a somber note. No one could suggest any effective way to

71. P.C.A. *Bulletin*, Vol. I, No. 20, May 1, 1918, Tamiment Institute; Peterson and Fite, *Opponents of War*, pp. 184-185; New York *Call*, May 24, 1918.
72. New York *Call*, May 1, 1918.
73. *Ibid.*, May 5, 1918.

break the Administration censorship except to send letters to personal friends in Europe.[74]

While the A.F. of L. and Alliance had been urged to provide labor's ambassadors of good will, and the Alliance had propagandized this role among the labor movement, the Council had to be content with a series of weak protest rallies. The pacifists had learned much about the suppression policies of a representative government during wartime. Although Wilson had made a bold gesture in the Fourteen Points toward making the world safe for democracy, the anti-war radicals learned that democracy at home did not necessarily apply to them.

Chapter 8. Labor's Ambassadors of Good Will

Although the Bolsheviks refused to accept Wilson's Fourteen Points as the basis for a final peace settlement, America's allies paid them lip service, and at home the President's program provided a powerful incentive to the loyalty movement. The Fourteen Points encouraged the working classes of the Allies and provided them with a program which could counter the peace propaganda of the Bolsheviks. It was during the summer of 1918, too, that America committed a significant number of troops to Europe, and the nation became more interested in those distant battlefields. This renewed public interest in the war was evidenced by the way the government pushed its war plans and by the C.P.I.'s expanded overseas bureau. Pacifism became increasingly unpopular at home, and anyone who worked against the war effort was subjected to rough treatment by the government, but more so by those whose relatives were fighting in Europe. These Americans wanted to forget dissidence and get down to the serious business of winning the conflict and establishing a lasting peace.

During this period (the summer of 1918) Maisel busily ran the Alliance on a shoestring budget, while Gompers handled the A.F. of L.'s most urgent affairs before leaving for London to attend the Inter-Allied Labor Conference. Maisel's chief problem

74. Nearing contended that the Wilson Administration was trying to destroy the radicals by isolating them from their friends in other countries (*ibid.*, May 6, 7, 1918).

was still how to raise enough money to propagandize for the Fourteen Points among the "radical" unions. The C.P.I. was no help; unfortunately Creel was continually in hot water with Congress for either spending too much, wasting too much, or, as had been the case most recently, recklessly criticizing the House Ways and Means Committee for cutting the President's budget.[1] Creel's criticism of the House committee immediately touched off more criticism of the way in which he was running the C.P.I.[2] As usual, Creel ordered his accounting office to tighten its spending until Congress had determined the C.P.I.'s appropriations. He did, however, approve raises for both Maisel and Chester Wright.[3]

But the situation was to get much worse for the Alliance. Congress cut the C.P.I.'s appropriations from $2,098,000 to $1,250,000.[4] Both Maisel and Gompers feared that Creel would now cut the Alliance's outlay even further. Shortly before departing for Europe, Gompers warned Creel that if the C.P.I. again reduced its commitments to the Alliance, "It will be necessary to wind up Alliance affairs." Maisel hurriedly followed up Gompers' letter with one of his own complaining about any further cuts in his organization's programs.[5]

Creel, however, offered Gompers little hope that the C.P.I. might continue to finance the Alliance as its labor agency and suggested that Maisel ask Roger Babson of the Industrial Relations Division to assume the responsibility of carrying the Alliance.[6] At the same time he wrote Maisel the bitter news that as of August 1 the C.P.I. would be forced to cease financing the Alliance. But in order to help Maisel as much as possible, Creel highly praised the Alliance to Babson: "I cannot speak too strongly of the splendid work done by this organization and its possibili-

1. New York *Call*, May 19, 1918. Creel also apologized for a speech he had made at the Church of the Ascension in New York City criticizing the House Rules Committee, Congress, and several officials for interfering with President Wilson's policies (Mann to Wilson, May 20, 1918, Wilson papers).
2. Creel, *Rebel at Large*, p. 193.
3. Creel to Lee, June 4, 1918; Byoir to Lee, June 6, 1918, C.P.I. papers, 1-A5.
4. Lorwin, *The American Federation of Labor*, p. 152.
5. Gompers to Creel, July 12, 1918, Gompers papers; Maisel to Creel, July 15, 1918, C.P.I. papers, 1-A1-26.
6. Creel to Gompers, July 17, 1918, C.P.I. papers, 1-A1-26.

ties of tremendous helpfulness in the problems that you are facing." He confessed to his friend James Baker that it grieved him to be forced to cut back some of the C.P.I.'s operations.[7] Creel's endorsement of the Alliance eventually encouraged Babson to place the organization under the Industrial Relations Division of the C.P.I.

With his funds coming now from this new source, Maisel attempted to plan a series of loyalty rallies for July and August. Because of his tight budget, Babson turned down many of Maisel's plans and reduced the distribution of Wright's pamphlet, "Bugle Calls for Labor," which was to be distributed widely throughout the United States.[8] Behind the scenes, however, Creel had suggested to Gompers that the Alliance might survive on less money if Chester Wright were allowed to direct the organization's propaganda work, and if much of that program were drastically reduced.[9]

It was at this moment, when the Alliance appeared to be a failing agency, that the A.F. of L. was asked to play an important role in the establishment of a labor loyalty press at Laredo, Texas. It was no secret that the Federation long had been cultivating good relations with South America's labor leaders. Since 1901 Santiago Iglesias and John Murray of the A.F. of L. had been working at this task in South America. A Pan-American Federation of Labor had been set up in November but had attracted little attention from either American labor circles or President Wilson.[10] Iglesias and Murray's work in South America had brought to their attention the activities of German propaganda agents in that area, especially in Mexico. Gompers immediately decided to send an A.F. of L. fact-finding mission to investigate these reports. On July 10 Gompers received a report from his

7. Creel to Maisel, July 17, 1918; Creel to Roger Babson, July 17, 1918; Creel to James H. Baker, July 18, 1918, *ibid.*

8. New York *Times*, Aug. 6, 1918; Maisel to Atwater, July 27, 1918; Maisel to Byoir, July 29, 1918, C.P.I. papers, 1-A6.

9. Creel to Gompers, July 19, 1918, C.P.I. papers, 1-A1-17; Wright to Byoir, July 31, 1918, *ibid.*, 1-A5.

10. Taft, *The A.F. of L. in the Time of Gompers*, "Pan-American Labor and the Mexican Revolution," pp. 320-333; Sinclair Snow, *Samuel Gompers and the Pan-American Federation of Labor* (Durham, N.C., 1965). The latter is a detailed study of A.F. of L.–South American labor relations.

mission which indicated that German agents were highly active below the border. He subsequently asked Creel and Secretary of Labor Wilson to confer over the situation,[11] and the President was hastily informed of the matter. President Wilson had received other reports of this German activity and was deeply disturbed about the situation.[12]

After deliberating with Creel, Wilson authorized the setting up of a labor loyalty press at Laredo under the auspices of the A.F. of L.; this was in keeping with Gompers' advice that he could make more friends for the United States in South America than any governmental agency.[13] Yet if the Administration were to direct this press openly, or if the A.F. of L. were to sponsor the program, the South American laborers might suspect that this was another American attempt to interfere in their domestic affairs. It was decided, therefore, that the logical agency to handle the loyalty press was the Alliance. On August 8 Gompers transferred from the A.F. of L. to the Alliance's treasury a sum of $25,000 to run the press. The money had been provided by the President.[14] In the meantime, Wilson set aside another $25,000 from his National Defense Fund to finance the adventure.[15] J. G. Phelps Stokes was given explicit orders to accept this money and spend it without "too close adherence to technicalities . . ."; and John Murray, who was to direct the operation, was informed that "Gompers, Creel, Maisel and Wright were to handle this."[16]

The press was set up at Laredo and was operated by Iglesias, James Ford, and Murray under the pretense of being an Alliance activity. But it was a useless adventure. For hardly had the presses started to roll when the Central Powers began to fall apart. On September 29 Bulgaria signed an armistice; Turkey took a similar action on October 20. Wilson realized now that the fall of Germany was not far off. When Germany later signed an armistice

11. Gompers to Creel, July 10, 13, 1918, C.P.I. papers, 1-A1-17.
12. Gompers to Wilson, July 19, 1918; Wilson to Creel, July 31, 1918, Wilson papers.
13. Gompers to Creel, July 30, 1918, C.P.I. papers, 1-A1-17.
14. Gompers to Stokes, Aug. 8, 1918, Stokes papers, Box 31.
15. Wilson, memorandum, Aug. 28, 1918, Wilson papers; Gompers to Creel, Aug. 8, 1918, Gompers papers.
16. Wright to Stokes, Sept. 12, 1918; John Murray to Frank Morrison, Sept. 16, 1918, Stokes papers, Box 31.

on November 11, the short-lived Laredo press adventure came to an end. Perhaps the real value of the press lay in Wilson's willingness to allow the Alliance to act as the Administration's "labor ambassador" of good will below the border.

While the Alliance was acting as a "front" in Laredo, Gompers prepared to leave for the Inter-Allied Labor Conference in London. The A.F. of L. chief was news wherever he traveled, but his presence in Europe at this time was widely recognized as that of an official representative of the American government. Gompers may have gone to London to represent the A.F. of L., but he also went to sell the President's Fourteen Points to Allied labor. Gompers had looked forward to speaking in Europe. "When the labor situation in our country was in a fairly satisfactory condition," he said, "I was convinced that the service I could render by going to Europe was more than I then could do at home."[17] The American socialists, however, rather half-heartedly hoped that this tour would make Gompers more aware of the views of Europe's socialists.[18]

Accompanying Gompers on the tour were W. J. Bowen, John Frey, Charles Baines, Edgar Wallace, and Guy Oyster of the A.F. of L. The group left the United States on August 16, 1918,[19] and unlike the A.F. of L.'s earlier mission in March, its Atlantic crossing was uneventful. Upon arriving in London, Gompers and his assistants plunged into a series of luncheons, banquets, and conferences with the leaders of British labor, while at home the Alliance faithfully covered their chief's every move.[20]

Gompers made it clear from the beginning of the Inter-Allied Labor Conference that he stood firmly behind Wilson's Fourteen Points and would refuse any suggestion that American labor cooperate in a peace movement based on the Bolshevik proposals. He insisted that Wilson's program be the chief cornerstone for any final settlement of the war.[21] Gompers' determined support

17. Gompers, *Seventy Years*, II, 408.
18. New York *Call*, June 25, 1918.
19. Gompers, *Seventy Years*, II, 410.
20. "Gompers Heads Delegation of Five for International Labor Conference in London" and "Gompers Heads Delegation to Inter-Allied Labor Conference," American Alliance press releases, copies in C.P.I. papers, 1-A7.
21. Gompers, speech, London, Sept. 10, 1918, Gompers papers.

of the President angered many anti-war delegates who accused him of "selling out to capitalism" and of being unaware of the consequences of a harsh peace with Germany.[22] Back in the United States he was severely criticized by the anti-war forces for placing Wilson's program above the needs of labor, for placing victory ahead of any just settlement of the war issue, and of trying to suppress labor "liberalism" in Europe. Gompers' mission, the New York *Call* declared, would accomplish much for the Administration, but little for labor in general.[23]

As Gompers left London and toured the Continent, he continued to back Wilson's program by refusing to compromise with the European socialists on any international peace movement.[24] He was so successful in propagandizing for the American cause that even the New York *Call* had to admit that his tour was of great value to the American war effort.[25] But whether or not the mission had any significant effect in changing the European socialists' attitude toward the war is uncertain.[26] There can be little doubt, however, that his presence in Europe aided the C.P.I. and the Alliance in demonstrating the importance of the A.F. of L. to the Wilson Administration. When all was said and done, the A.F. of L.'s missions abroad showed Wilson's confidence in conservative labor and his need of organized labor's support abroad.

Upon his return to the United States, Gompers was welcomed in Chicago at a special Alliance reception similar to that held in St. Paul for the March mission. To aid Maisel in financing the reception, Creel contributed funds from the C.P.I.'s treasury.[27]

22. Kellogg and Gleason, *British Labor and the War*, p. 302; Gankin and Fisher, *The Bolsheviks and the World War*, p. 607.

23. New York *Call*, Aug. 14, 26, 29, Sept. 13, 1918.

24. Burton J. Hendrick, *The Life and Letters of Walter H. Page* (New York, 1922), II, 387-388. The A.F. of L.'s March mission had drawn high praise from Page.

25. New York *Call*, Sept. 22, 1918.

26. Austin Van Der Slice, *International Labor Diplomacy and Peace* (Philadelphia, 1941), pp. 286-288. Van Der Slice believes that the labor missions were too much under the control of the American government to have been very effective. On the other hand, L. L. Lorwin acknowledges that these missions did something in combating pacifist propaganda among Allied labor (*The A.F. of L.: A History*, p. 154).

27. Maisel to Byoir, Sept. 28, 1918, C.P.I. papers, 1-A6. Maisel requested an additional $1,000 for the reception after Creel already had given him $4,000 (Maisel and Creel, telegram, Nov. 4, 1917, *ibid.*).

But Gompers' appearance in Chicago was a sad one for him. His only daughter, Sadie, had died unexpectedly, and he was in a period of deep depression. Yet he spoke eloquently about his tour to an assembly of eleven state governors, Frank Walsh of the War Labor Board, and the A.F. of L.'s delegates. The reception was a propaganda success. The state governors and a large contingent of Chicago businessmen rubbed shoulders with the laborites, while the Chicago Chamber of Commerce staged a large banquet for all those present.[28]

During the time that Gompers toured Europe for the Wilson Administration, Maisel was forced to run the Alliance at home on a tight budget. On July 14, Bastille Day, he transmitted dozens of congratulatory telegrams from the A.F. of L. unions to French labor; and that night he staged a Bastille Day rally in Madison Square Garden in honor of the French workers.[29] Thereafter, Maisel directed the usual rallies, bond drives, and organizing campaigns, but on a much smaller scale than before. The chief organizing effort, however, again centered on the anti-war Jews on the East Side. Creel feared that those Jews, recently arrived from Russia, might still be sympathetic to the Bolsheviks and might resist the efforts of the government to "Americanize" them. The Bolsheviks were admired among many of these people who remembered only too well the recent persecutions of the Tsar's government. Creel and Maisel worked to build another Jewish loyalty agency which would play up the participation of America's older Jewish elements in the war effort. The agency was to be named the Jewish Loyalty War Committee, and Maisel was chosen as director. In the first meeting at the McAlpin Hotel in New York City, William Edlin, editor of *The Day*, was elected secretary.[30] Creel had instructed Maisel to be sure that he impressed upon the committee the need to propagandize among the "proRussian" Jews on the East Side.[31] But the C.P.I.'s plans soon hit a snag. After attending one of the meetings, Creel was bitterly

28. New York *Times*, Oct. 27, 1918; Wright to Walsh, Oct. 3, 1918, Walsh papers, Box 24; Gompers, *Seventy Years*, II, 473; Maisel to Creel, Oct. 19, 1918, C.P.I. papers, 1-A1-6.
29. New York *Times*, July 14, 1918.
30. Maisel to Creel, Sept. 7, 1918, C.P.I. papers, 1-A1-26.
31. Maisel to Creel, Oct. 2, 1918, *ibid.*

disappointed at the lack of response which the committee had received from the Jews. In an attempt to revitalize the movement, he sought the services of Rabbi Stephen S. Wise of the Alliance, who never failed to exert a strong influence upon the moderate Jewish element.[32]

But the war was drawing to a close and there was a general realization among the Jews that Germany was near collapse. Each day the country's newspapers hailed Germany's defeats and the Allies' successes; the President had been notified secretly on October 22 of the imminent fall of Germany's military government.[33] Ten days later the public learned of a mutiny in the German naval yards at Kiel and of the Kaiser's flight to Holland. There is little wonder that during these weeks loyalty work was forgotten. The plans for the Jewish Loyalty War Committee were abandoned as the country awaited the fall of Germany.

Meanwhile, the anti-war radicals of the Peoples Council had faced some of their most serious problems. First, there was the arrest of Scott Nearing for writing "The Great Madness." The Council, however, proclaimed Nearing's arrest as the beginning of a government campaign to stamp out radicalism. The radicals noted the debate in Congress over universal military training and declared that a permanent army would be used to suppress radicalism at home. Likewise, they were suspicious of conscription, which they asserted was the first step toward establishing a military tradition that could be used by the government to suppress dissidents.

The Administration's arrest of Nearing and everyone else who attacked conscription did not discourage the socialists and pacifists from opposing the draft. Indeed, they launched a "holy crusade" against those who talked of universal military training, and they openly encouraged America's young men not to obey their government's call to arms.[34] The Administration took a dim view of this "obstructionism," and Postmaster Burleson restricted all anti-conscription propaganda from the mails. Burleson's campaign was so effective that Lochner was forced to call a special Council meeting at New York's Central Opera House to ask members to distri-

32. Creel to Wise, Oct. 15, 1918, *ibid.*, 1-A1-45.
33. House to Wilson, Oct. 22, 1918, Wilson papers.
34. Lochner to all Council members, May 1, 1918, Swarthmore; P.C.A. *Bulletin*, Vol. I, No. 18, April 1, 1918, Tamiment Institute.

bute their anti-conscription literature in person or mail it in unmarked envelopes.[35]

The Council's notoriety increased. Members like Alexander Trachtenberg attended meetings of the pro-Bolshevik Russian-Soviet Recognition League, and John Reed, recently returned from Russia, traveled all over the East Coast speaking in favor of the new Soviet regime.[36] In addition, the Council's ally, the Socialist party, began to co-operate with the same movements.[37] Eugene Debs, never an active Council member but who was nevertheless on the rolls, was arrested at Canton, Ohio, as he bitterly attacked the Administration for "zig-zagging in curves for the master class." Debs's anti-conscription pamphlet, "Never Be A Soldier," already had been distributed widely by the party and the Council.[38] His subsequent trial, his defense by Seymour Stedman and Morris Hillquit, and his sentence to ten years in federal prison, all added to the extremist image of the Council and the Socialist party.

The international situation also intensified the Council's woes. By August the Allies had actively intervened in the Russian civil war, and the United States had committed an expeditionary force to Siberia largely to counter the influence of Japanese troops in that area.[39] For American socialists and pacifists, however, the issues were clear: the United States was aiding the Allies in a "capitalistic" attack upon a government created by the Russian working people. As a result, at a time when the American public was becoming fearful of the revolutionary threat of Bolshevism, the Socialist party in its Chicago convention asked its members to support the "gallant struggle of the Russian people" for self-determination; while socialists in New York held a rally where John Reed appealed for aid to "free Russia."[40] Earlier, the Council had demanded that the Wilson Administration accept the

35. Lochner to Council members, April 2, 1918, Swarthmore.
36. New York *Call*, June 5, 1918.
37. *Ibid.*, June 9, 1918. The Socialists in Boston were among the first to extend recognition to the Bolsheviks.
38. *Ibid.*, July 2, 1918; Eugene Debs, "Never Be a Soldier," published by the Socialist party, copy, Tamiment Institute; Ginger, *The Bending Cross*, pp. 353-356; Debs, speech, Canton, Ohio, June 16, 1918, copy, Tamiment Institute.
39. Wilson, statement, Jan. 16, 1920, cited in Shaw, ed., *Messages and Papers of the Presidents*, XVII, 8824-8826.
40. New York *Call*, Aug. 14, 15, 1918.

Russian peoples' right to determine their own government in the "spirit of the Russian labor movement."[41]

But the Wilson Administration had no intention of recognizing the Bolsheviks or of pulling America's troops out of Siberia. As far as Secretary Lansing was concerned, Bolshevism was the "most hideous and monstrous thing that the human mind has ever conceived,"[42] and if allowed to win out in Russia, it would certainly spread throughout Western Europe.[43] Concerned over the number of Bolshevik organizations springing up in the United States, Creel wrote Attorney General Gregory of the need for further action against this menace. John Reed, Creel asserted, was "the head and center of the movement in this country."[44]

Reed was only one of the many radicals who had begun to shy away from the moderate leadership of Hillquit to support those societies which were imitating the Bolsheviks. Despite Hillquit's support of the Russian peoples' right to self-determination, the leftists, led by Louis Fraina and Louis Boudin, started their own communist splinter groups, while the Socialist party in Boston became a hotbed of pro-revolutionary radicalism. Many socialists joined with the radical Friends of Russia and the Russian Federation.[45] The socialist left-wingers became so vocal that Meyer London, congressman from New York's East Side, had to restate his party's moderate position in the House of Representatives. London's efforts were fruitless, however, for he could not persuade his peers that the party had not swung over to Bolshevism.[46] Hillquit, faced with a serious schism between the moderates and leftists, had tried desperately to hold the party together.[47] He publicly announced that the socialist position would be a moderate one, as it had been in the past. The party had never been a revolutionary

41. P.C.A. *Bulletin*, Vol. I, No. 21, May, 1918, Tamiment Institute.
42. Lansing, "Memo on Absolutism and Bolshevism," private memorandum, Lansing papers.
43. Lansing, confidential memorandum, "Memo on Post-Bellum Conditions," *ibid*.
44. Creel to Attorney General Gregory, Oct. 28, 1918, C.P.I. papers, 1-A-17.
45. Bell, "Background and Development," pp. 319-320.
46. *Congressional Record*, House of Representatives, 65th Congress, second session, July, 1918, p. 5909; Harry Rogoff, *An East Side Epic* (New York, 1930), pp. 104-109, 167.
47. Hillquit to Harriman, June 28, 1918, Hillquit papers.

movement, Hillquit asserted.[48] But the arrest of John Reed at a Russian "friendship" rally in Hunt's Point Casino did not help the party's image. And when Debs's conviction made the headlines, it appeared that the party had come under the influence of the left-wing faction.[49] Earlier, the Socialist party and the Council had been labeled communist "front" organizations in a magazine article by Lewis Allen Browne.[50]

With public hysteria mounting over Bolshevism within the United States, Council officials faced insurmountable problems in raising funds for their organization. As early as April, Lochner complained that the censorship of the mails was so complete that he could mail scarcely a single letter.[51] When voluntary donations fell off to a trickle in July, he cut expenses to a miminum and ordered the *Bulletin* printed on a bi-monthly basis.[52] The Socialist party faced the same problems, and Hillquit ordered a halt to the printing of a handbook because "the mails are so suppressed I don't believe it is worth the money."[53] The censorship was so tight that by the latter part of August Lochner informed the Executive Committee it would be necessary to wind up the Council's activities "at least temporarily, because of increasing debts and the inability to correspond with the general public."[54] Moreover, Scott Nearing informed Lochner that he planned to seek the socialist nomination in New York's Fourteenth District congressional race and would have to devote his full time to the campaign.[55]

After much deliberation, Lochner decided to close down the Council, for it was apparent in October that the organization would never build a "social democracy" in America. Lochner was left with nothing but the shadow of an organization. Never-

48. Hillquit to Root, Aug. 12, 1918, *ibid.*
49. New York *Call*, Sept. 13, 1918. Both Debs and Reed were arrested under the Espionage Act for spreading sedition (*ibid.*, Sept. 15, 1918).
50. Lewis Allen Browne, "Bolshevism in America," *Forum*, LIX (June, 1918), 703-717.
51. Lochner to all Council members, April 27, 1918, Swarthmore.
52. P.C.A. *Bulletin*, Aug. 1, 1918, Vol. I, No. 23, Tamiment Institute.
53. Hillquit to Germer, Aug. 4, 1918, Hillquit papers.
54. Lochner to Executive Committee, P.C.A., Aug. 26, 1918, Swarthmore. Lochner listed Council debts at this time as $1,335 and loans borrowed as $1,859.
55. New York *Call*, Aug. 27, 1918. Nearing lost the election (*ibid.*, Nov. 7, 1918).

theless, Elizabeth Freeman declared that she was not going to abandon the council movement and would seek some "prominent personage" to take over the organization.[56] But the telegrams which she wired to her friends were sent under the name of the Peoples Council, and immediately the wireless operators turned them over to the Justice Department.[57] With the council movement effectively censored by the government, Lochner announced his decision to shut down the organization:

> The Post Office Department, by holding up our literature, had rendered it impossible for us to carry on an effective mail propaganda. Everywhere our active locals have been raided, many of them have been broken up; practically all of them have been forced to suspend active work . . . our failure to engage in any large activity was not due to inertia on our part.[58]

By the end of October, the Council began to disband. It had failed to arouse the American worker to the need of a quick negotiated peace and a "social democracy." Likewise, the Alliance was a failing organization. But for the A. F. of L. the decline of the Alliance was not a serious situation. By October, 1918, the Alliance had served its purpose of opposing pacifist-socialist propaganda in the labor movement and of demonstrating the A.F. of L.'s loyal support of the government. Gompers believed that its loss now would not damage the respectable image which the A.F. of L. had carefully built for its labor movement.

Chapter 9. The Reconstruction Period: A Setback

The German armistice of November 11, 1918, came as no immediate surprise to either Wilson or Gompers. It had been apparent since Bulgaria and Turkey had left the war that Germany could not long survive. The summer, too, had witnessed the last great offensive by the imperial armies to crash through the Allies' de-

56. Freeman to Dana, Oct. 15, 1918, Dana papers: "I do not plan to join the Socialist Party and thus I find myself alone."
57. Freeman to Dana, Oct. 20, 1918, *ibid.*
58. P.C.A. *Bulletin*, Vol. I, No. 24, Sept.-Oct., 1918, Tamiment Institute.

fenses. Its eventual failure turned the scales against the Central Powers and broke the stalemate which had kept the German armies poised in northern France. As a member of the Advisory Commission of the Council for National Defense, Gompers had realized that the immediate collapse of Germany was not far distant. But the A.F. of L. chief had lost some of his previous optimism that labor would be able to hold its wartime position during the postwar period. Now that peace was near, Gompers wondered if business would accept labor's wartime gains. Then too, he was disturbed lest the government drop its relatively paternal policy now that labor's co-operation was no longer essential.[1] It was not the President about whom Gompers was most concerned, but those members of Congress who were sympathetic to the business community—those who during the war had been content to co-exist with labor for the sake of national unity. Gompers also was worried about the speed with which the Administration was closing down those agencies like the War Industries Board which had been sympathetic to labor's problems.[2] All in all, Gompers would have felt more comfortable if he had had a little more time to build the A.F. of L. as a responsible labor movement.[3]

The fading Alliance now took on added importance in his eyes. If there were to be a reaction against labor, the Alliance might be needed to propagandize the A.F. of L. cause before the public. As Maisel was winding up the Alliance's business, he received a letter from Gompers suggesting that the organization might be useful during the postwar period to keep the public informed on labor's determination to be a responsible part of society.[4] Even the knowledge that the A.F. of L. would be allowed to send representatives to the coming peace talks at Versailles did not ease Gompers' fears that the Federation might not continue to keep the government's confidence.[5]

The future of the Alliance was uncertain; Creel was closing

1. Clarkson, *Industrial America*, p. 280. Clarkson had approved the government's attitude toward labor.
2. Blum, *Joe Tumulty and the Wilson Era*, p. 180.
3. Norman Thomas related that Gompers was heard to remark on November 11, 1918, that he had wished for more time to build his labor movement before the war ended (interview with Thomas, July 7, 1964, New York City).
4. Gompers to Maisel, Nov. 27, 1918, Gompers papers.
5. New York *Call*, Dec. 2, 1918.

down the C.P.I. offices and there was no guarantee that the Alliance could be adequately financed by the A.F. of L.[6] The Federation already had discovered that its efforts to raise money for propaganda purposes had not proved successful. Nevertheless, the Executive Committee met in the Continental Hotel on November 30 to discuss the future of the organization. Maisel informed the committee that his final report would show that the Alliance "had been helpful in defeating socialism and pacifism" in the conservative labor movement. However, it was not the wartime role of the Alliance which now concerned these officials; they were interested in Gompers' suggestion that the Alliance might be useful to the A.F. of L. in the postwar period. This proposal was fully debated, and the committee members agreed to re-establish the Alliance as the A.F. of L.'s propaganda agency. They reasoned that the Alliance, as a symbol of labor "loyalty," might well serve a useful purpose during the critical reconstruction period, and they heartily endorsed Gompers' suggestion that the Alliance continue functioning.[7]

The committee then set about determining what the Alliance's peacetime program should be. Ernest Bohm, who had been one of the original founders of the Alliance, declared that the organization should continue to unite the A.F. of L. with its socialist friends. It also should oppose the profiteering that was bound to rise once governmental controls were removed, he asserted, and propagandize for the maintenance of high wages and the preservation of labor's wartime benefits. Bohm believed that the Alliance could still utilize the "loyalty issue" by standing firm against revolutionary movements such as the Bolsheviks.[8] W. R. Gaylord, who had worked for the Alliance in the Midwest, asserted that loyalty work was still needed there because of the thousands of immigrants who were receptive to Bolshevism. Likewise, Chester Wright feared the rise of Bolshevism in the East; but Frank Wolfe of the A.F. of L. agreed with Gompers that the most important

6. Creel to Tumulty, Nov. 27, 1918; Creel to Henry Atwater, Nov. 14, 1918, C.P.I. papers, 1-A1-1. Creel wrote, "Make all arrangements for the Division of Production and Distribution to go out of business by January 1, 1919."

7. Executive Council report, American Alliance, Continental Hotel, Nov. 30, 1918, Gompers papers.

8. *Ibid.*, p. 2.

peacetime job of the Alliance would be to aid the A.F. of L. in holding its own against management.[9]

Interestingly enough, the Alliance's pro-war socialists led by Stokes and Spargo went along with these proposals. Spargo declared that the Alliance could perform a valuable service by cooperating with the loyal socialists who were concerned about democracy in America.[10] Spargo's reasons for staying with the Alliance may well have stemmed from his need for more time to build his own movement; certainly the pro-war socialists had little to gain by allying themselves with the Alliance except to use that organization as a "front" for their own movement. After much discussion, all agreed that the peacetime Alliance should oppose labor "radicalism," maintain labor's wartime gains, oppose profiteering, work for effective labor representation in the government, and act as an A.F. of L. propaganda agency.[11] This program was announced officially the next day.[12]

Gompers, Spargo, and Maisel carried this program to the rank-and-file at the Alliance's armistice celebration in the Century Theatre. Maisel was the first to speak and pledge that the 175 unions for which he spoke would aid the A.F. of L. in every way possible to maintain labor's wartime standards. When someone in the audience cried out that the National Founders Association had suggested that labor could not expect to maintain its wartime gains during the postwar period, Gompers leaped to his feet and declared: "What the devil does Mr. Barr [of the National Founders Association] and his type think we have made all these sacrifices for?" Gompers angrily warned the audience, "Already the reactionaries are at work to undermine the wartime gains of labor." But, he shouted, "The workers will prevent these industrial barons from riding horseback over the masses!" His denunciation of those who insisted that labor return to its prewar status drew thunderous applause from the assembly.[13]

9. *Ibid.*
10. *Ibid.*, p. 3.
11. *Ibid.*
12. New York *Times*, Dec. 1, 1918.
13. *Ibid.*, Dec. 2, 1918. Gompers informed the Senate Committee on Education and Labor that labor would not gracefully accept cutbacks or unemployment. At the same time, Scott Nearing predicted the end to the labor-management alliance in "Winter of Gloom," New York *Call*, Jan. 5, 1919.

Gompers' hopes for the new Alliance, however, soon received some serious setbacks. Frank P. Walsh, long a champion of liberal reform and a man greatly respected by all factions of labor, resigned from the organization. At a time when Gompers hoped to rally the support of the liberal unions against the business community, this resignation was unfortunate, for it implied that the Alliance was not the organization to represent the views of American labor.[14]

Walsh's disillusionment with the conservative philosophy of both the Wilson Administration and the A.F. of L. was apparent when he resigned from the National War Labor Board in November over what he considered the Administration's favoritism toward big business.[15] His particular quarrel with the Alliance had reached a climax when that organization published a series of articles written by Gustavus Myers attacking the Bolshevik government of Russia. Walsh, believing that the Russian people should have the right to determine their own government, remarked that Wilson's malice against the revolution was "a vicious onslaught on a whole body of people fighting to control their destiny."[16] He informed Gompers that because of "pressing business obligations" he could no longer devote his time to the Alliance. Although Gompers realized that Walsh's resignation would severely damage the Alliance, he calmly replied, "Of course if you resign after we have decided to continue our work with a reconstruction program there is nothing for me to do but accept your resignation."[17] When informed of the resignation, Maisel remarked, "I did not expect such a mild resignation from Walsh because of his dissatisfaction with our attitude toward the Bolsheviks."[18]

Walsh's resignation from the Alliance was only one of its problems. Shortly after Gompers had departed for Europe to take

14. Walsh had continued to hold some sympathy for socialism while serving with the Administration. His article, "Democracy or Destruction," appeared in the *Young Socialist's Magazine*, Vol. XII, Nov., 1918, and had been well received by the editor: "No socialist will find anything wrong with Mr. Walsh's statements" (copy, Socialist Party papers, Duke University).

15. New York *Call*, Nov. 20, 1918. Walsh wanted to see the government do more to break up monopolies.

16. Walsh to Wolfe, Dec. 30, 1918, Walsh papers, Box 26.

17. Gompers to Walsh, Dec. 31, 1918, Gompers papers.

18. Maisel to Gompers, Jan. 2, 1919, *ibid.*

part in the international labor conferences at Versailles, a general strike broke out in Seattle.[19] Although the A.F. of L. was not enthusiastic about supporting the strikers, many of whom were leftists, the Federation went along with its unions in that area. Mayor Hanson chose to believe that the strikes had been inspired by American communists and declared publicly that the workers were attempting to "set up a revolutionary government." Although the A.F. of L. asserted that the strikes were caused by layoffs and wage reductions, this assertion did little to ease the minds of those who saw behind every labor strike the shadow of the Bolsheviks.[20]

Maisel, who believed that the Alliance was urgently needed to publicize the A.F. of L.'s side of the story, hurriedly went about soliciting funds for this propaganda. Matthew Woll, on the other hand, believed that Maisel's appeal for funds would make the A.F. of L. appear to be soliciting support, and as a member of the Executive Committee he wired Gompers for his opinion.[21] When informed of Maisel's actions, Gompers ordered the director to stop soliciting. But Maisel was closer to the situation than Gompers, and he replied that he hoped the A.F. of L. chief would be prepared for the increased number of attacks upon labor when he returned to the United States. He warned Gompers that unless money was forthcoming, he could not keep the Alliance operating.[22] To help ease the pressures on the A.F. of L., Gompers declared as he left France that no communists would gain a foothold in the conservative labor movement.[23]

Gompers arrived in the United States during the opening

19. Taft, *The A.F. of L. in the Time of Gompers*, p. 438. Gompers was asked to serve on the International Labor Commission on January 21, 1919 (Gompers, *Seventy Years*, II, 478-479). When informed of the appointment, Oswald Villard remarked that Gompers was a Wilson man and could not be counted upon to represent all labor factions (Michael Wreszin, *Oswald Villard: Pacifist At War* [Bloomington, Ind., 1965]) p. 97.

20. New York *Call*, Feb. 3, 16, 1919. An objective study of the Seattle general strike which finds little radical influence in the movement is Robert L. Friedheim, *The Seattle General Strike* (Seattle, 1964).

21. Woll to Gompers, cablegram, Feb. 26, 1919, Gompers papers.

22. Maisel to Gompers, March 14, 1919, *ibid*. The Alliance later obtained $3,000 of the money left over from the Laredo press venture. Creel authorized the transfer (Gompers to Stokes, July 8, 1919, *ibid*.).

23. New York *Call*, March 30, 1919.

phases of that mass hysteria over Bolshevism often called the "Red Scare."[24] The public had become suspicious of the increased number of strikes throughout the country following the return to peace, and it was especially alarmed by the Seattle general strike which seemed to have touched off this unrest.[25] As rumors circulated that a substantial number of communists had infiltrated the A.F. of L., public hysteria mounted. The socialists had always been accused of harboring Bolsheviks, but now the Federation was suspected of turning to communism as a way of achieving further labor gains. Moreover, numerous bomb packages had been sent through the mails of eight different cities, and most of these bombs had been addressed to those same business and governmental officials who had been critical of labor.

For many Americans the only answer to this threat lay in the "Americanization" of American labor. Ironically, the A.F. of L. now was attacked by the same organizations which had previously co-operated with the Alliance. The National Security League, the National Defense Society, and the National Civic League, all dominated by businessmen, demanded a purge of the A.F. of L.'s rank-and-file until every "communist" was ousted.[26] The hysterical fear of Bolshevism in labor's ranks stretched from New York State, where the legislature set up a committee under Clayton Lusk to investigate radicalism, to the halls of Congress where Senator Overman of North Carolina led a vigorous investigation of radicalism on the national level. In Washington, Attorney General A. Mitchell Palmer asked Congress for $500,000 to rid the country of "extremists."[27] The fear of Bolshevism was so strong that Secretary of State Lansing suggested that the country must prepare to "meet a coming revolution."[28]

Against this background, the A.F. of L. acted "loyally" at its convention in Atlantic City. The delegates refused to endorse the Soviet regime or call for the lifting of the Allied blockade of Russia. For his part, Gompers spoke out against radicalism in

24. *Ibid.*, April 23, 1919.
25. Robert K. Murray, *The Red Scare* (Minneapolis, 1955), pp. 79-80.
26. See Murray's chapter, "The Patriotic Defense," *ibid.*, pp. 82-104, for the role of the business community in the Red Scare.
27. New York *Call*, June 11, 13, 1919.
28. Lansing, confidential memorandum, July 26, 1919, confidential memoranda, Lansing papers.

labor and pledged that he would do all that was necessary to purge any delegate who displayed even a hint of radicalism.[29]

After the convention Gompers, hoping that a new directorship could help it survive, ordered a complete reorganization of the Alliance. Maisel was forced to resign, and Matthew Woll succeeded him. Gompers' lack of confidence in Maisel's leadership had started when the director had solicited funds without consulting the Executive Committee. There also had been much discontentment in the committee with Maisel's erratic and often individualistic leadership. Even Spargo and Stokes had suggested a reorganization of the directorship; and Chester Wright, one of the most even-tempered committee members, had declared that he could "no longer work with the present director."[30] At an executive conference in the Continental Hotel on July 1, Maisel resigned to pave the way for Woll to become director. Chester Wright moved up as chief assistant to the director, and Stokes remained as treasurer.[31] With the reorganization complete, Gompers again sailed for Europe to attend the National Trade Union Conference at Amsterdam.[32]

The A.F. of L.'s opportunity to build a powerful labor movement by co-operating with the government and with capital had suffered a setback. As early as December, 1918, Gompers had urged the National Civic Federation to support labor's right to maintain its wartime wages. At the same time he had informed the Executive Committee of his optimistic view that the business community would accept the Federation's reconstruction program.[33] Indeed, it appeared that Gompers' appointment by Wilson to the International Labor Commission at Versailles indicated a continued acceptance of labor's position.[34] At Versailles Gompers had faithfully supported Wilson's program during those hectic labor negotiations, and he had stood firm against allowing the

29. New York *Call*, June 18, 19, 1919.

30. Stokes to Gompers, June 2, 1919; Wright to Gompers, June 24, 1919, Gompers papers.

31. New York *Times*, July 12, 1919; Gompers to Morrison, July 13, 1919, Gompers papers.

32. New York *Call*, July 12, 1919; Taft, *The A.F. of L. in the Time of Gompers*, p. 433.

33. Gompers, address, National Civic Federation, Dec. 2, 1918; speech, Labor Reconstruction Conference, Dec. 7, 1918, Gompers papers.

34. Gompers to Wilson, cablegram, Dec. 21, 1918, *ibid.*

Bolsheviks a place in the conference.[35] He had backed the President when many of the A.F. of L.'s liberal unions had charged that Wilson had compromised America's war aims to old world autocracy.[36] For his loyal stand, Gompers had received a letter of appreciation from Secretary of State Lansing.[37]

A leader of lesser determination might have grown discouraged because of the attacks on the A.F. of L.; but Gompers was a realist. He firmly believed that the A.F. of L.'s alliance with the government since 1912 had been a wise one and that organized labor could not have acted otherwise. Since the vast majority of the Federation's unions continued to support the government, Gompers once again fell back on a consensus policy and continued to steer a conservative course. This was as it should have been, for the Federation's immediate problem was one of survival and how to maintain those benefits that it already had gained.

After Gompers' return from Amsterdam, the A.F. of L. faced another serious crisis—a nationwide strike against United States Steel. At St. Paul in June, 1918, the Executive Committee had authorized the Federation to direct the unionization of the steel industry. William Z. Foster, an outspoken syndicalist, had been appointed secretary of the committee charged with directing the campaign. At this time, Gompers saw no reason to block Foster's appointment, for Foster seemed no more "radical" than the hundreds of extremists with whom Gompers had established a working relationship. In August the committee presented Judge Elbert H. Gary, chairman of United States Steel, with the A.F. of L.'s demands for an eight-hour day, higher wages, and other benefits. Gary refused to accept the demands, and shortly thereafter more than 343,000 workers walked out of his plants. The strike soon spread to other steel companies, and by September the situation had become one of the country's major peacetime problems. United States Steel fought the strikers by bringing in strikebreakers, hir-

35. Gompers, memorandum, Paris, Jan. 30, 1919, *ibid.*; Morrison to Wilson, Feb. 25, 1919, Wilson papers.

36. A.F. of L. Executive Committee to Wilson, telegram, June 26, 1919, Wilson papers. The telegram endorsed the League of Nations. Gompers urged all A.F. of L. unions to support the League (Lee Girard to Tumulty, July 17, 1919, *ibid.*)

37. Lansing to Gompers, Paris, Sept. 1, 1919, Gompers papers.

ing its own armed guards, and spreading rumors that the strike had been planned and carried out by "left-wingers" within the A.F. of L.

Public fear of communism was so great at this point that many Americans accepted the strike as a prelude to a workers' revolution. Consequently, Foster's presence on the strike committee, which had seemed advisable to Gompers in June, now, with the loss of the public's confidence, proved an embarrassment that Gompers gladly would have done without. The A.F. of L. could not back down; it already had committed itself to organizing the steel industry, and any other course would have severely weakened the Federation.[38] With the impossible task of supporting the rank-and-file, and at the same time preserving what was left of the A.F. of L.'s position as a powerful labor federation, Gompers wrote John Frey in discouragement about the need for labor officials who would stick to the necessities of the moment and not idealize about unobtainable goals.[39]

As Gompers struggled with the steel strike problem, the President, who already had carried the burden of the Versailles negotiations and now was engaged in pushing the treaty through the Senate, stepped into the crisis and offered to mediate the dispute. The President called for a series of White House conferences in October,[40] but his health was failing and he could not always follow the negotiation proceedings.[41] For a brief time it appeared as if the President might force United States Steel to accept the A.F. of L.'s demands. However, Wilson no longer controlled Congress, and he had to be cautious in backing the Federation or face the possibility of alienating a large number of congressmen vitally needed to support the Versailles Treaty.[42]

The White House conferences opened in early October in an atmosphere of open hostility. The United States Steel representatives were determined not to compromise their position, while Gompers was compelled to stand firm for the demands of the

38. Taft, *The A.F. of L. in the Time of Gompers*, p. 389.
39. Gompers to Frey, Sept. 3, 1919, John Frey papers.
40. New York *Call*, Sept. 23, 1919.
41. Wilson, memorandum, Sept. 3, 1919, Wilson papers.
42. Gompers was disappointed that the Council of National Defense would not direct the reconstruction of labor (Lombardi, *Labor's Voice*, pp. 304-305).

unions.[43] With both sides taking an unbending position, the first meeting failed to produce any significant results. The New York *Call* reported that Gompers had suggested a truce during the negotiations, but Judge Gary had refused the offer.[44] Gompers had hoped that the President might mediate the impasse, but the ailing Wilson remained too preoccupied with the Versailles Treaty to devote his full attention to the steel negotiations.[45] The second conference went as badly as the first. Gompers was irritated by press support of the steel industry and its attacks on the A.F. of L.'s position. At one point in the negotiations, he angrily criticized the adverse influence of the "present national hysteria" on the conferences, referring to accusations that Foster was one of the "leftists" being sheltered by the A.F. of L., and stubbornly walked out.[46]

While the steel strike negotiations dragged on, the public hysteria over Bolshevism in the country mounted. If the American people were convinced that the communists had succeeded in infiltrating organized labor, they were equally convinced that the only way to stop this infiltration was to suppress labor radicalism wherever it could be found. Already the Clayton Lusk Committee and the Overman Committee had held dozens of sessions to determine how to accomplish this suppression. The most obvious place to find "radicals" was of course in the Socialist party and its affiliated organizations. The Peoples Council, like the A.F. of L., thus had its own particular problems of survival.

Shortly after the November 11 armistice, Council officials, who previously had decided to disband, suddenly became interested in pressuring Congress to accept the Bolsheviks in the peace negotiations. Before a new program could be gotten under way, however, Lochner thought it better to resign and allow those who had not

43. Hundreds of letters poured into A.F. of L. headquarters urging Gompers not to give in to United States Steel (Sept. 10–Oct. 6, 1919, copies in Gompers papers). The New York *Times*, Sept. 30, 1919, reported that Gompers would refuse to concede anything to the steel industry.

44. New York *Call*, Oct. 10, 1919.

45. Gompers, *Seventy Years*, II, 516. Gompers wrote, "Wilson had just started to secure popular support in favor of the treaty ratification" (*ibid.*, p. 517).

46. *Ibid.*, p. 517. Gompers believed Foster to be a liberal, but not actually a communist. However, he had begun to have suspicions of Foster's real objectives in directing the steel strike.

been so directly identified with "radicalism" to take over the movement.[47] His offer was turned down by the Executive Committee. The committee then set about drawing up a peacetime program which called for the repeal of the espionage and sedition acts, the release of those "political prisoners" who had been arrested for criticizing the government, and the acceptance of the Bolshevik regime in Russia. Furthermore, the Council urged the Administration to support the entry of the Bolsheviks into the League of Nations so that the working classes of the world might be represented.[48] The Socialist party had advocated a similar program and had sought to elect delegates to the International Labor Conference at Versailles, although there was no guarantee that they would be allowed to attend.[49]

Both the socialists and the pacifists were in for a continued difficult time, however, for peace did not bring them toleration. Nearing's efforts to distribute his new pamphlet, "The Soviets at Work," was barred from the mails by Postmaster General Burleson at the same time that the Alliance announced its intentions of fighting "radicalism" during the postwar period.[50] The situation worsened when five socialist leaders, including Victor Berger, St. John Tucker, and Adolph Germer, were indicted in Chicago for sedition. This trial is interesting because former Alliance members Frank P. Walsh and Clarence Darrow both testified for the defendents, while John Spargo testified against his former friends.[51] Nor were the radicals allowed any freedom in New York, where both John Reed and Max Eastman were barred from directing a Russian friendship rally on the East Side.[52]

Meanwhile, the Overman Committee in the Senate continued its own investigations of "radical" activity in the United States. The sensational evidence, some of it clearly biased, that was presented during these hearings did much to prevent the Administra-

47. Lochner to Executive Committee, P.C.A., Nov. 21, 1918, Swarthmore.
48. This program was based on an earlier one, adopted on November 9, to "set up a program for democracy and reconstruction" (Executive Committee to H. W. L. Dana, Nov. 1, 1918, Dana papers).
49. New York *Call*, Nov. 2, 1918.
50. *Ibid.*, Dec. 3, 1918.
51. *Ibid.*, Dec. 5, 20, 22, 27, 1918.
52. *Ibid.*, Jan. 9, 11, 1919.

tion from easing up on the anti-war forces. Archibald E. Stevenson, an investigator for the committee, charged that Emily Balch, H. W. L. Dana, Elizabeth Freeman, Hillquit, Jordan, Keasbey, Lochner, Magnes, Maurer, Nearing, Debs, Panken, Norman Thomas, and Schlossberg had willingly used the Socialist party and the Peoples Council (the Council was always referred to as being an extremely dangerous organization) to spread "pro-German" propaganda throughout the United States.[53] To make the evidence even more incredible, Stevenson mentioned Lillian Wald and Jane Addams as radicals of a similar stripe.[54] On February 14, when the committee turned its attention to investigating Bolshevik propaganda in the United States, both the Socialist party and the Council were mentioned as agents for Bolshevism in America.[55]

Lochner did not allow these investigations to prevent him from pushing the Council's peacetime program. Fully aware of the public temper, he nevertheless spoke at the Central Opera House for Russia's right to be represented in the League; later at the Broadway Casino he condemned the "closed door negotiations" taking place among the Big Four at Versailles.[56] Even as the public followed the conclusion of Nearing's trial for writing "The Great Madness," Lochner spoke out in Brooklyn for the right to criticize the government during peacetime.[57] Two days later, Lochner was among those who met at the Peoples House to set up the famous Civil Liberties Bureau, an agency which was given the task of defending American "radicals" against government suppression.[58] At the same time Lochner remained in touch with Nearing, who was touring for the Rand School's educational program for socialism.[59] Lochner also joined with the Socialist party to raise money for Eugene Debs's release from prison,[60] and he directed a rally

53. "Extracts of the Testimony of Archibald E. Stevenson Before the Overman Committee," Jan. 21-22, 1919, compiled by Ernest L. Meyer, copy, Swarthmore; New York *Call*, Jan. 23, 1919.

54. New York *Call*, Jan. 28, 1919.

55. *Ibid.*, Feb. 15, 1919.

56. *Ibid.*, Feb. 7, 8, 1919.

57. *Ibid.*, Feb. 20, 21, 1919.

58. *Ibid.*, Feb. 23, 1919.

59. On March 4, Lochner led the Rand School chorus at a victory celebration for Nearing after his acquittal for sedition. The event was held in the Yorkville Casino (*ibid.*, March 5, 1919).

60. *Ibid.*, March 23, 1919.

at the Yorkville Casino to protest the continued arrest of "radicals" under the wartime Espionage Act.[61]

The Council, too, distributed a pamphlet, "Workers Stand Up for Your Rights," along with several others, "Democracy and Peace," and "The Madness at Versailles," in an attempt to arouse public opinion against what the pacifists considered Wilson's betrayal of his wartime promises to create a world democracy.[62] Although the propaganda was generally ignored, its message was a telling one. For these radicals feared the consequences of a harsh peace treaty on Germany and the failure of the League to accept the Bolsheviks.[63] The Council sought to get its propaganda to the public by asking its members to carry the literature from door to door.[64] That propaganda which did get distributed, however, only added to the public's fear of "radicalism"; and on May Day, 1919, there was an unprecedented outburst against extremists. In New York an angry group of servicemen raided the Rand School and roughed up those inside. The New York *Call*'s offices were likewise raided, and in Cleveland May Day demonstrators were protected from the mobs only by the use of troops.[65]

Despite this angry public mood, the Council did not let up its efforts to pressure the Wilson Administration to accept the Russian government. On May 25 the pacifists sponsored a rally in Madison Square Garden on behalf of the Russian revolution. Precautions were taken to prevent trouble by forbidding the red flags of socialism to be displayed by the crowd. Nevertheless, large numbers of people milled outside the Garden and pushed against the lines which the police had set up to keep back troublemakers.

61. Robert Lovett of the *Dial*, John A. Fitch of the *Survey*, and Don Seitz of the *World* spoke with Lochner, who charged Gompers with giving up the fight for labor standards. See Lochner, speech, March 29, 1919, copy, New York Public Library.

62. "Workers of the World Stand Up for Your Rights" and "Democracy and Peace," publications; Scott Nearing, "The Madness at Versailles," publication, New York City, Jan., 1919, copies, Tamiment Institute.

63. T. A. Bailey, *Woodrow Wilson and the Great Betrayal* (New York, 1945); George Kennan, *American Diplomacy, 1900-1950* (Chicago, 1953), p. 68. Kennan discusses the effects of the Versailles Treaty on the future peace of Europe.

64. Lochner to Hull, April 9, 1919. Lochner asked Hull to recommend a list of people willing to distribute Nearing's pamphlet, "Is Violence the Only Way Out?" (letter and pamphlet in P.C.A. file, Swarthmore).

65. New York *Call*, May 2, 1919.

Inside, the radicals often could not contain themselves and cheered whenever the names of Lenin and Trotsky were mentioned by Frederick C. Howe of the United States Commission of Immigration. Howe called for the lifting of the Allied blockade and an end to America's interference in Russia's civil war. For his part, Rabbi Magnes pleaded with the Administration to understand better the Russian people's desire to set up their own government.[66] The rally ended with the assembly pledging itself to pressure the Wilson Administration to abandon its attempts "to stamp out the Bolshevik government."[67]

The socialists found themselves seriously hampered in working for the recognition of the Russian people, however, for once again the party was torn apart by a schism. The extreme left wing, under the guidance of Louis Fraina, William Bross Lloyd, and John Reed, decided to take over the leadership of the party.[68] The publicity surrounding this split called the public's attention to the large numbers of leftists within the socialists' ranks and seriously weakened the party's efforts to carry out its peacetime objectives. The Council as an ally of the socialists was also adversely affected by this publicity.[69] Thus, the revival of radical propaganda in the mails, the increased number of rallies supporting the Bolsheviks, and those mysterious bomb packages which appeared throughout the country, all brought the hysteria to a peak during the summer of 1919.

The Wilson Administration did not wait for the radicals to unite in their actions against the government. Attorney General Palmer immediately undertook a vigorous campaign to stamp out "radicalism" before it could crystalize into a revolution.[70] Palmer

66. *Ibid.*, May 26, 1919; P.C.A. *Bulletin*, Vol. II, No. 6, June, 1919, Swarthmore.

67. John Holmes, speech, Madison Square Garden, May 25, 1919, Tamiment Institute.

68. Theodore Draper, *The Roots of American Communism* (New York, 1957), "The Real Split," pp. 148-163; Bell, "Background and Development," pp. 320-323. The Hillquit papers contain a number of interesting letters between Adolph Germer and Hillquit prior to the Chicago convention at which the party threw out the left-wingers. See also Eastman, *Love and Revolution*, p. 163. Eastman was an observer.

69. Thomas to Jordan, June 10, 1919, Thomas papers, Box 4; interview with Thomas, July 7, 1964.

70. Frederick Palmer, *Newton D. Baker*, II, 197, 205. Eastman refers

used all the forces at his command to suppress the Friends Of
Russia, the Union Of Russian Workers, the Socialist party, and
the Council.[71] Whether Palmer truly believed he was preventing a
revolution, or whether he was simply paving his own way to the
White House, is uncertain. The total effect of his campaign, however, was devastating to the radical cause.[72] Fear of radicalism
was taken so seriously that even Wilson's personal secretary, Joseph Tumulty, who had been a champion of conservative labor,
now shied away from any endorsement of the A.F. of L.[73]

Still the Council continued to demand its rights to speak. On
June 7 it held a protest rally in Madison Square Garden for the
release of Eugene Debs from prison, during which Panken, Berger,
Algernon Lee, and Nearing boldly addressed a crowd of some
six thousand persons.[74] On June 21 the Rand School was again
raided, but this time it was done by investigators for the Lusk
Committee who were searching for proof that the school was a
revolutionary "front" organization.[75] Although Lee fully co-operated with the intruders and allowed them to search the files, the
investigators confiscated the material and transported it to the
committee's offices. Shortly thereafter the committee announced
that the Socialist party and the Council were involved in spreading
subversion.[76]

The Palmer raids, combined with the Lusk Committee hearings, had a profound effect on the Council's ability to continue
functioning. Across the country the Council's locals were raided,
their files seized, and the mails tightly closed to their propaganda.
By August the *Bulletin*'s circulation had dropped by more than
one hundred thousand copies. With funds running out and the
mails closed, Lochner decided to discontinue the *Bulletin* in Au-

to the "madness of the Palmer raids" and of the courage needed to speak
for "radicalism" in those days (*Love and Revolution*, p. 144).

71. Stanley Coben, *A. Mitchell Palmer: Politician* (New York, 1963),
pp. 218-219.

72. Frederick Palmer, *Newton D. Baker*, II, 197. Palmer writes that
Attorney General Palmer "slew the liberal dream" (p. 220). He also states
his belief that the Attorney General's motives were political.

73. Blum, *Joe Tumulty and the Wilson Era*, p. 191.

74. New York *Call*, June 8, 1919.

75. *Ibid.*, June 22, 1919.

76. Murray, *The Red Scare*, pp. 101-102; Lusk *Report*, I, 1076. The
radicals called a "defense for the Rand School" meeting on July 10, 1919
(New York *Call*, July 10, 1919).

gust.[77] The New York *Call*, too, was having its own problems with the Administration's censorship and struggled to operate by reducing the frequency of its editions.[78]

The public now was solidly behind the Administration's efforts to stamp out "radicalism." While Palmer's agents raided nationally, and the Lusk Committee locally, socialists, pacifists, and liberals of all shades were arrested for being subversives. The public and many congressmen no longer could tell the difference between a "liberal" and a "radical." In the midst of this national hysteria, the Council finally gave up trying to operate. Faced with the difficulties of government suppression, a lack of funds, and a failing membership, Lochner and the Executive Committee decided that the organization no longer could serve a useful purpose. Some time in October, 1919, the Council disbanded and its members melted into the Peoples Freedom Union, which had been formed to work for the release of those jailed for sedition.[79]

Ironically, the Council's antagonist, the Alliance, also was struggling against the same fate. Chester Wright found it increasingly difficult to convince the public that the A.F. of L. was not sheltering Bolsheviks.[80] Like Lochner, Wright was faced with terrible problems, among them public apathy and a serious lack of operating capital.[81]

Meanwhile, the atmosphere continued tense as a result of the failure of negotiations to end the paralyzing steel strike. Gompers and the Federation came under increasing attack for not calling off their campaign against the steel industry. Shortly thereafter the press turned on Gompers himself, accusing him of "bowing

77. P.C.A. *Bulletin*, July-Aug., 1919, Vol. II, Nos. 7-8, Tamiment Institute.

78. New York *Call*, July-Aug., 1919. The *Call* was desperate for circulation and funds at this time.

79. Lusk *Report*, I, 1105. The New York *Call* (Aug. 19, 28, 31, Sept. 10, Nov. 9, 10, 1919) records the number of former Council members in the Peoples Freedom Union. Scott Nearing to author, Oct. 26, 1960: "Any organization taking the Council's stand was in for a rough time. Patriotic support for the war was widespread and general." Max Eastman recalls that when he first joined the Council in 1917 he realized that "those who tried to prevent the war would be crushed . . ." (*Love and Revolution*, p. 57).

80. "Don't Lower the Standard of Living During Reconstruction," American Alliance publication, Gompers papers.

81. Chester Wright to author, Feb. 16, 1960.

to the will of a small group of revolutionaries" within the Federation. On the floor of Congress where he had once been praised for his loyalty, Gompers now was charged with condoning communism in the A.F. of L. He discouragingly lamented before the Executive Committee: "And so here we are. We are beset by those who would strike at our very organization. But we must carry out the labor movement. . . . Times are more critical than at any other period in the history of our country!"[82]

The steel impasse continued into January, 1920, before the Federation finally admitted defeat and called off the strike. Subsequent investigations of this episode cleared the A.F. of L. of any subversive charges and upheld Gompers' contention that the steel industry underpaid and overworked its men.[83] Nevertheless, the strike had done untold harm to the Federation's image as a respectable labor organization. By January the public regarded it only with suspicion.

The Alliance, which had been caught up in these critical events, had tried vainly to publicize the A.F. of L.'s point of view. Several rallies were held during the fall in Spokane, Pittsburgh, Toledo, and St. Paul. For a while the New York *Times* forgot its recent anti-labor position and praised the Alliance for its opposition to labor "radicalism";[84] but the A.F. of L.'s funds were depleted by the steel strike and the payment of union benefits. The Alliance's treasury was soon depleted, too. When Chester Wright made a hurried attempt to solicit money (with Gompers' permission), he failed to bring in more than three or four hundred dollars.[85] Under the circumstances, Wright and Woll decided to disband the Alliance late in November. In March, 1920, Chester Wright received the following letter which might serve as an epitaph for the A.F. of L.'s loyalty organization: "We are sorry to hear of the Alliance's suspension. Your material has been of value to the labor press."[86]

82. Executive Committee, A.F. of L., Gompers speech, Dec. 13, 1919, Washington, D.C., Gompers papers.
83. Bishop Francis J. McConnell, *Report of the Steel Strike of 1919* (New York, 1920), pp. 245-51. McConnell, *Public Opinion and the Steel Strike* (New York, 1921), "Radicalism Disloyalty, and Un-Americanism," pp. 101-110.
84. New York *Times*, Sept. 2, 1919.
85. Wright to Gompers, Oct. 25, 1919, Gompers papers.
86. Brown to Wright, March 4, 1920, *ibid.*

The nation was concerned with "normalcy," and "normalcy" meant, in part, returning labor to its prewar status. The A.F. of L.'s co-operation with the nation's war effort, its fight against labor radicalism, were forgotten. The long road toward respectability would have to be traveled at a later time.

Conclusion

Shortly after the news of the German armistice had reached the United States, Gompers reportedly remarked to one of his secretaries that the A.F. of L. had needed more time to consolidate its wartime gains. World War I had presented the Federation with an unprecedented opportunity to gain the respect of the government and the business community. Indeed, World War I had been the first American war which had offered the Federation this opportunity. The A.F. of L. had been an infant organization during the Spanish-American War and was considered relatively unimportant by the McKinley Administration. Moreover, the vast majority of the Federation's membership had become involved in the emotional desire to free Spain's colonies from her imperialistic rule. And although the A.F. of L. was suspicious of America's true desires when she took over the majority of Spain's colonies, the Federation did little to demonstrate its dislike of the final treaty.

The pacifist organizations of that day were equally as weak as the A.F. of L. Pacifism made little headway against the emotional demand of the American public to free the Spanish colonies. There was, too, no new foreign ideology, as in 1917, to excite the pacifists and send them on a world crusade for international brotherhood. The country had adopted a war policy and had carried out that policy in record time.

The situation in 1914 was far different. World War I was a complex and confusing episode in world history. The issues were not clear, although Wilson tried to make them so. The Federation now had a membership of almost thirteen million. Similarly the Socialist party had gained a record vote of approximately one million in 1912. The party made rapid gains after the United States embarked on its colonial course in 1898. Socialists and radical unions made good progress in organizing the immigrant elements of the industrial Northeast and the rural Midwest, areas which later proved vital to the American war effort.

In April, 1917, the Administration was faced with the problem of keeping labor loyal to the war effort and resistant to the obstructionist programs of the socialist-pacifist bloc. This task was complicated by the American people, who were confused over the causes of the war. Wilson attempted to end this confusion by making the war effort a crusade for world democracy, but the anti-war forces refused to endorse this idealistic concept of American policy. The radicals were suspicious of Great Britain's rank as the world's greatest commercial power and of France as the hereditary enemy of Germany. Nor did the radicals sympathize with the totalitarian government of the Russian Tsar, who was well-known for his persecution of socialists and Jews.

After American entry into the war, the majority of the Federation's unions loyally supported the government. But the socialist-pacifist anti-war bloc was making good progress in infiltrating the war industry in the Northeast and the Midwest. The Federation's leadership had not forseen this threat, nor had the Wilson Administration. When the Bolsheviks of socialist Russia became vocal enough to advance a peace plan in November, 1917, and the American President had none, the situation became serious.

It was at this point that the American Alliance was formulated by the Central Federated Union of New York City and the A.F. of L. to propagandize against the obstructionist arguments of the Peoples Council. Since the Administration needed a labor pacification program at this time, Wilson placed the Alliance under the financial arm of the Committee on Public Information. The Alliance became an important agency to the A.F. of L. because it represented a joint Federation and Administration function. The opportunities presented the A.F. of L. were vast, and the leadership intended to make the best of them. The Alliance became a supernationalistic organization intent on co-operating fully with the government's war program. The war and the Alliance thus presented the A.F. of L. with an unprecedented opportunity to advance its programs.

After the pro-war socialists expressed an interest in working with the Alliance, the A.F. of L. sought to divide the Socialist party permanently by drawing off part of the party's membership. Hence the Alliance was to have been an alliance, too, between conservative and liberal labor. But by placating the Administration with supernationalism, the Alliance frightened away numerous liberals who feared the loss of their identity if they co-operated with the organization. The Alliance failed in its efforts to "Americanize" the liberal labor elements, and its best efforts were made in aiding the Administration to keep conservative labor behind the war effort.

When the war ended and the Alliance was dropped by the government, the Federation attempted to keep the organization active by incorporating it as a propaganda wing. The country's mood, however, was changing. The "Red Scare" was now real, or at least many in the Administration thought so. That same nationalistic wave of hysteria which the Alliance had helped perpetrate during the war was turned against the Federation as the public saw labor filled with Bolsheviks. The Alliance idea perished as the A.F. of L. declined in popularity. If the Alliance had succeeded in gaining a rapproachement between the Federation and the pro-war radicals, the American labor movement might have been enriched at an early date with a dynamic liberal element.

Despite the failure to unite the conservative and the liberal in labor, the Alliance opposed the Peoples Council effectively. Nevertheless, all of the Council's objectives were not unsound. While the country supported Wilson's crusade for democracy, the Council pointed out time and again that a lasting peace could not be built without the aid of socialist Russia. When in 1918 the Wilson Administration sent American troops to Russia, the Council and the Socialist party warned, to no avail, that this action would cause Russia to become an enemy of the United States. Likewise, the anti-war radicals believed that the Treaty of Versailles would establish a world community of nations, but as Wilson compromised his high ideals the radicals foresaw the final treaty as a guarantee that Germany would seek to regain by force her former position of power. A study of the Council's minutes and the papers of Hillquit, Nearing, and Lochner reveals that they possessed an accurate knowledge of world affairs. The Council and the Socialist party wanted Germany returned to her former position of power. Total defeat of Germany, they asserted, would be a disaster for the world community.

Domestically, the Council was not afraid to call for a more progressive labor movement. Council leaders pointed out that the business community was too powerful at that time for the A.F. of L. to follow a cautious program of gradualism. They accused Gompers of being too willing to co-exist with capitalism for a conservative labor movement to make any significant progress. The labor movements of Western Europe had moved beyond a cautious program, and as a result, the Council leaders asserted, the governments of England, France, and Italy had granted significant concessions to their workers. Moreover, the radicals argued that the A.F. of L.'s co-operation with the government would bring only limited concessions from the capitalistic system. The American worker would have to demand progress before any progress could be made. But the suggestions of the Council and the Socialist party were ignored as the public panicked over Bolshevism and the Wilson Administration became entangled in domestic and international policies.

The tragedy of the era can be summed up in the opportunities missed by the American people. Germany was disgraced, Russia had become deeply suspicious of the United States, and the American labor movement had experienced a sharp reversal during the postwar period. The Alliance and the Council were small voices crying for significant changes in a wilderness of complacency. The American nation chose to label these cries as those of a radical minority; the country set forth on a more moderate and safer course.

Years later the American people once again called upon the worker's loyalty in fighting a severe depression and in winning a second world war. In the process, the Democratic party helped gain for labor a series of reforms never dreamed of by Gompers. Likewise, the American government embarked again on a course of international responsibility. The international temper of the nation would have warmed the heart of the most ardent Peoples Council member. By 1946 the American nation had committed itself to continued labor reform and continued international responsibility—two goals for which the Alliance and the Council had struggled in their separate ways back in 1919.

Manuscripts

Much of the material pertaining to the American Alliance for Labor and Democracy has been lost or widely scattered throughout many manuscript collections in the United States. The largest single collection of the Alliance papers, however, can be found in the Samuel Gompers Papers and Copy Books in the American Federation of Labor Archives, Washington, D.C. The Gompers papers contain several hundred letters, pamphlets, and memoranda in the American Alliance files, but more importantly there are even more letters scattered through the general Gompers correspondence. This material numbers over 10,000 pieces and requires much effort to investigate. The Copy Books also contain some Alliance material, which is located according to date and year. The New York Public Library has some Alliance propaganda on file and a few letters.

The second most important source of Alliance material is the Committee on Public Information papers, Diplomatic and Fiscal Division, National Archives, Washington, D.C. Sections 1A5-1A26 contain a great deal of correspondence between George Creel, representatives of his division, and the Alliance directors. Creel's General Correspondence, however (1A1), is disappointing. The C.P.I. papers contain some of the few remaining financial statements of the Alliance.

The John Frey papers in the Manuscript Division of the Library of Congress contain some correspondence between Gompers and Frey concerning Alliance business. The collection is small, however, and pertains mostly to the period after 1920.

John Spargo's papers housed at the Vermont State Agricultural University in Burlington are important because they contain some important letters to Gompers, J. G. Phelps Stokes, and Robert Maisel of the Alliance. The Spargo collection is small, and, unfortunately, some material has been destroyed.

The J. G. Phelps Stokes papers at Butler Library, Columbia University, New York City, are very enlightening. Some material, such as that pertaining to Stokes's early radicalism, has been destroyed, but most of the Alliance correspondence remains, including some financial statements. These papers were used with the permission of Mr. Stokes, and after his death, Columbia University.

Limited are Frank P. Walsh's papers, most of which can be found under the Committee on Industrial Relations, 1917-1919, in the Manuscripts Division of the New York Public Library. But there are several important letters here which reveal Walsh's opinion of Gompers, the Alliance, and conservatism in general.

The papers of President Woodrow Wilson, Manuscript Division, Library of Congress, are of great importance to the historian interested in labor history during World War I. The most interesting letters are those between Gompers and Wilson concerning labor radicalism. There is little correspondence directly with the Alliance, but Wilson's letters and memoranda to and from George Creel are valuable. These papers were used with the permission of Mrs. Wilson, and after her death, the Library of Congress.

Robert Lansing's correspondence gives some insight into the government's fears of the Bolsheviks abroad and the anti-war radicals at home. "Confidential Memoranda and Notes," January 2 through December 27, 1919, contain his personal opinion of the Bolsheviks. The Lansing papers, some sixty-two volumes, concern primarily official correspondence. The Desk Diaries, volumes I-V, are Lansing's personal day-by-day appointment pads and are of little value here.

Postmaster Burleson's letters of 1917 to 1919, arranged according to year, contain some material pointing out the government's role in the censorship of the mails. Many of these letters refer to Council pamphlets and officials.

Group 60, of the Justice Department Files, National Archives, contains some reports on the department's investigations of the anti-war radicals. But much of this material is closed to the public.

The Postmaster General's papers, Group 28, Social and Economic Division of the National Archives, are very valuable to an understanding of the censorship problems of the government. Many of these letters were mailed directly to the Justice Department for investigation.

It was hoped that the following collections would contain a great deal of material pertaining to the Alliance and its problems, but unfortunately they contained little of value. The material in Group I, the General Records of the Department of Labor, concerned general labor problems of strikes, layoffs, negotiations, etc., but little on the problems of radicalism. The Thomas W. Gregory papers in the Library of Congress likewise contained little or nothing concerning the Alliance. The A. Mitchell Palmer papers in the Library of Congress were a great disappointment in this area, for the material was concerned mostly with intra-party political affairs. Moreover, the William B. Wilson papers in the Pennsylvania State Historical Society referred primarily to matters of a non-radical nature: the Alliance was hardly mentioned.

The largest single collection of material on the Peoples Council of America for Democracy and Terms of Peace can be found in the Swarthmore Peace Collection, Swarthmore College, Swarthmore, Pennsylvania. This is one of the finest collections on pacifism in the country, and the librarians make it a pleasure to do research there. The material in the collection on the Council is of vast importance. There are financial statements, minutes of the various committee meetings, and an almost complete collection of the very scarce *Bulletin*. Included among the Peace Collection's manuscripts which pertain to the Council are the Jane Addams papers, the papers of the American Union Against Militarism, the Emily C. Balch papers, and the Henry Wadsworth Longfellow Dana papers, which hold a great deal of correspondence concerning the Council's problems. The papers of the Woman's Peace Party, and the William I. Hull papers both give an interesting insight into the style in radical correspondence of the day.

The State Historical Society of Wisconsin in Madison houses the Morris Hillquit papers, which are disappointing because most of the material concerns the Socialist party and not Hillquit's Council activity. Likewise, the Seymore Stedman papers are a very small collection, and most of the Council correspondence has been destroyed.

Stanford University's large collection of material on war, revolution, and peace, contains the David Starr Jordan papers, which are of much interest concerning Jordan's contacts with numerous pacifist movements—including the Council.

The Socialist party papers at Duke University are the largest single collection in the country, but they pertain mostly to the period after 1920. There is some party correspondence with Council officials and some financial material which does not exist elsewhere.

The Tamiment Institute Library, New York City, houses a large collection of material on radicalism. The library has many Council *Bulletins* which cannot be found at Swarthmore, but it has little of the Council's correspondence. There is much pacifist propaganda material here, however, and the Eugene Debs file is of interest.

The Norman Thomas papers (used with the permission of Mr. Thomas) have some material dealing with the Council and numerous pacifists, but over-all they do not contain a great deal on activities before 1920. The New York Public Library will not open these papers without special permission from Mr. Thomas. The library also houses the American Civil Liberties Union papers on microfilm, which may be used within the library only. The Lillian Wald papers housed here are not much help on matters concerning the Council.

The Ford Peace Mission papers may be of interest to those scholars dealing with the pacifist period before 1917, when many of the Council's later members worked with Ford to try for a negotiated peace. They may be found in the Library of Congress.

One of the greatest disappointments was the Paul U. Kellogg *Survey* papers just acquired by the University of Minnesota. At this writing they had not been catalogued and were not available to the general public. But correspondence with the library and its research staff made it clear that most of the material pertaining to the Council activity of the *Survey* has been destroyed.

Works Cited

Books and Articles

Addams, Jane. *Peace and Bread in Time of War*. New York: Kings Crown Press, 1945.

Allen, Devere. *The Fight for Peace*. New York: Macmillan, 1930.

Anon. "The Kaiser's Secret Army Here." *Literary Digest*, LV (Dec. 1, 1917), 15-16.

———. "Pacifist Pilgrims." *Literary Digest*, LV (Sept. 15, 1917), 16-17.

————. "The Socialist as Patriot." *Literary Digest*, LV (June 16, 1917), 36-37.

Bailey, T. A. *Woodrow Wilson and the Great Betrayal*. New York: Macmillan, 1945.

Baker, Ray Stannard. *Woodrow Wilson: Life and Letters*. Vols. I-VIII. New York: Doubleday, 1937.

Blum, John. *Joe Tumulty and the Wilson Era*. Boston: Houghton-Mifflin, 1951.

Bourne, Randolph S. *War and the Intellectuals: Collected Essays, 1915-1919*, ed. Carl Resek. New York: Harper, 1964.

————. *Towards an Enduring Peace: A Symposium of Peace Proposals and Programs, 1914-1916*. New York: American Association of International Conciliation, 1927.

Browne, Lewis Allen. "Bolshevism in America." *The Forum*, LIX (June, 1918), 703-717.

Bruere, Robert. "Labor and the New Nationalism." *Harper's*, LVI (April, 1919), 746-752.

Bunyan, James, and H. H. Fisher. *The Bolsheviki Revolution*. Stanford: Stanford University Press, 1934.

Burns, E. M. *David Starr Jordan: Prophet of Freedom*. Stanford: Stanford University Press, 1953.

Carr, Edward H. *The Bolsheviki Revolution*. Vols. I-II. New York: Macmillan, 1951.

Clarkson, C. B. *Industrial America in the World War: The Strategy Behind the Lines, 1917-1918*. New York: Houghton-Mifflin, 1923.

Coben, Stanley. *A. Mitchell Palmer: Politician*. New York: Columbia University Press, 1963.

Cole, Margaret. *Beatrice Webb's Diary*. Vols. I-II. London: Longman, 1952.

Conkin, Paul K. *Two Paths to Utopia: The Hutterites and Llano Colony*. Lincoln: University of Nebraska Press, 1964.

Cramer, C. H. *Newton D. Baker: A Biography*. New York: World, 1961.

Creel, George. *How We Advertised America*. New York: Harper, 1920.

————. *Rebel at Large*. New York: G. P. Putnam's Sons, 1947.

Cronon, David, ed. *The Cabinet Diaries of Josephus Daniels, 1913-1921*. Lincoln: University of Nebraska Press, 1963.

Curti, Merle. *Peace or War: The American Struggle.* New York: W. W. Norton & Co., 1936.

Darrow, Clarence. *The Story of My Life.* New York: Scribners, 1934.

Draper, Theodore. *The Roots of American Communism.* New York: Viking Press, 1957.

Eastman, Max. *Love and Revolution: My Journey Through an Epoch.* New York: Random House, 1964.

―――. *Reflections on the Failure of Socialism.* New York: Devin-Adair, 1955.

Egbert, D. D., and Stow Persons, eds. *Socialism and American Life.* Vols. I-II. Princeton: Princeton University Press, 1952.

Epstein, Memech. *The Jews and Communism.* New York: Trade Union Sponsoring Committee, 1959.

Fine, Nathan. *Labor and Farmers' Parties in the United States, 1828-1928.* New York: Rand School, 1928.

Foster, William Z. *From Bryan to Stalin.* New York: International Publications, 1937.

―――. *Misleaders of Labor.* New York: Trade Union Educational League Publication, 1927.

―――. *The Russian Revolution.* New York: Trade Union Educational League Publication, 1955.

Friedheim, Robert L. *The Seattle General Strike.* Seattle: University of Washington Press, 1964.

Gankin, Olga Hess, and H. H. Fisher. *The Bolsheviks and the World War.* Hoover Library on War, Revolution, and Peace, No. 15. Stanford: Stanford University Press, 1960.

Ginger, Ray. *The Bending Cross.* New Brunswick, N.J.: Rutgers University Press, 1949.

Goldman, Emma. *Living My Life.* Vols. I-II. New York: Knopf, 1931.

Goldmark, Josephine. *Impatient Crusader.* Urbana: University of Illinois Press, 1953.

Gompers, Samuel. *Seventy Years of Life and Labor.* Vols. I-II. New York: G. D. Doran Co., 1919.

―――. *American Labor and the War.* New York: G. D. Doran Co., 1919.

Harvey, Rowland H. *Samuel Gompers: Champion of the Toiling Masses.* Stanford: Stanford University Press, 1935.

Hendrick, Burton J. *The Life and Letters of Walter Hines Page.* Vols. I-III. New York: Doubleday, 1922.

Hillquit, Morris. *Loose Leaves from a Busy Life.* New York: Macmillan, 1934.

Houston, David F. *Eight Years with Wilson's Cabinet.* Vols. I-II. New York: Doubleday, 1926.

Hull, William I. *Preparedness: The American vs. Military Programme.* New York, 1916.

Hutchinson, William T. *Lowden of Illinois.* Vols. I-II. Chicago: Chicago University Press, 1957.

Johnson, Donald. *The Challenge to American Freedom: World War I and the Rise of the Civil Liberties Union.* Lexington: University of Kentucky Press, 1963.

Jones, J. P., and P. M. Hollister. *The German Secret Service in America.* Boston: Small, Maynard & Co., 1918.

Jordan, David Starr. *The Days of a Man.* Vols. I.-II. New York: World, 1922.

Josephson, Matthew. *Sidney Hillman: Statesman of American Labor.* New York: Doubleday, 1952.

Karson, Marc. *American Labor Unions and Politics, 1900-1918.* Carbondale: Southern Illinois University Press, 1958.

Kellogg, Paul U. "Socialists and Unionists Hang Together." *The Survey,* Sept. 22, 1917, p. 558.

————, and Arthur Gleason. *British Labor and the War.* London: Boni and Liveright, 1919.

Kennan, George. *American Diplomacy, 1900-1950.* Chicago: University of Chicago Press, 1953.

Kipnis, Ira. *The American Socialist Movement, 1892-1912.* New York: Columbia University Press, 1952.

La Follette, Belle Case, and Fola La Follette. *Robert M. La Follette.* Vols. I-II. New York: Macmillan, 1953.

Laidler, Harry W. *Socialism in Thought and Action.* New York: Macmillan, 1925.

Land, Harry, and Morris Feinstone. *Gewerkschaften.* New York: United Hebrew Trades Publication, 1938.

Lang, Lucy Robins. *Tomorrow Is Beautiful.* New York: Macmillan, 1948.

Lansing, Robert. *War Memoirs.* New York: Bobbs-Merrill, 1935.

Lasch, Christopher. *The American Liberals and the Russian Revolution.* New York: Columbia University Press, 1962.

Leonard, A. R., ed. *War Addresses of Woodrow Wilson.* New York: Ginn, 1918.

Leuck, Miriam Simons. "The American Socialist and Labor Mission to Europe, 1918: Background Activities and Significance, an Experiment in Diplomatic Diplomacy." Unpublished Ph.D. dissertation, Northwestern University, 1941.

Link, Arthur S. *The American Epoch.* New York: Knopf, 1959.

————. *Woodrow Wilson and the Progressive Era.* New York: Harper, 1954.

————. *Wilson: The Road to the White House.* Vol. I. Princeton: Princeton University Press, 1954.

————. *Wilson: The Struggle for Neutrality.* Vol. III. Princeton: Princeton University Press, 1960.

————. *Wilson: Confusion and Crisis.* Vol. IV. Princeton: Princeton University Press, 1964.

Linn, W. James. *Jane Addams.* New York: Appleton, 1930.

Lochner, Louis P. *Henry Ford: America's Don Quixote.* New York: International Publishers, 1925.

————. *Always the Unexpected.* New York: Macmillan, 1956.

Lombardi, John. *Labor's Voice in the Cabinet: The History of the Department of Labor from Its Origin to 1921.* New York: Columbia University Press, 1942.

Lorwin, L. L. *The American Federation of Labor.* Washington, D.C.: The Brookings Institute, 1933.

————. *The International Labor Movement.* New York: Harper, 1953.

————. *Labor and Internationalism.* New York: Macmillan, 1929.

Lusk, Clayton R. *Revolutionary Radicalism: Report of the Joint Legislative Committee of the State of New York.* Vols. I-IV. Albany: J. B. Lyon, 1920.

Mandel, Bernard. *Samuel Gompers: A Biography.* Yellow Springs, Ohio: Antioch Press, 1963.

Martin, Franklin H. *Digest of the Proceedings of the Council of National Defense During the World War* (73rd Congress, Senate, second session, Document No. 193). Washington: United States Government Printing Office, 1934.

Maurer, James H. *It Can Be Done*. New York: Rand School, 1938.

McConnell, Francis, Bishop. *Report of the Steel Strike of 1919*. Bureau of Industrial Research. New York: Harcourt, Brace, 1920.

————. *Public Opinion and the Steel Strike*. New York: Harcourt, Brace, 1921.

Mock, James R., and Cedric Larson. *Words That Won the War: The Story of the Committee on Public Information, 1917-1919*. Princeton: Princeton University Press, 1939.

Mowat, Charles L. *Britain Between the Wars, 1918-1940*. Chicago: University of Chicago Press, 1961.

Murray, Robert K. *The Red Scare*. Minneapolis: University of Minnesota Press, 1953.

O'Neal, James. "The Socialist in the War." *American Mercury*, April, 1927, pp. 418-426.

Osgood, Robert E. *Ideals and Self-Interest in American Foreign Policy*. Chicago: University of Chicago Press, 1953.

Palmer, Frederick. *Newton D. Baker: American at War*. Vols. I-II. New York: Dodd, Mead, 1931.

Pares, Bernard. *History of Russia*. New York: Knopf, 1947.

Paxson, Frederick L. *America at War*. Vols. I-III. Boston: Houghton-Mifflin, 1939.

Peterson, Horace, and Gilbert Fite. *Opponents of War*. Madison: University of Wisconsin Press, 1957.

Preston, William, Jr. *Aliens and Dissenters: Federal Suppression of Radicals, 1903-1933*. Cambridge: Harvard University Press, 1963.

Reed, John. *Ten Days that Shook the World*. New York: Modern Library, 1935.

Reese, Albert. *The Economics of Trade Unionism*. Chicago: University of Chicago Press, 1962.

Rischin, Moses. *The Promised City: New York Jews, 1870-1914*. Cambridge: Harvard University Press, 1962.

Rogoff, Harry. *An East Side Epic*. New York: Vanguard, 1930.

Saposs, David J. *Left-Wing Unionism*. New York: International Publishers, 1926.

Seymour, Charles, ed. *The Intimate Papers of Colonel House*. Vols. I-IV. New York: Houghton-Mifflin, 1926.

Shannon, David A. *The Socialist Party of America: A History.* New York: Macmillan, 1955.

Shaw, Albert, ed. *Messages and Papers of Woodrow Wilson.* Vols. I-II. New York: Review of Reviews, 1924.

Snow, Sinclair. *Samuel Gompers and the Pan-American Federation of Labor.* Durham, N.C.: Duke University Press, 1965.

Soule, George. *Sidney Hillman.* New York: Macmillan, 1939.

Spargo, John. *America and Social Democracy.* New York: Harper, 1918.

Stolberg, Benjamin. *Tailors' Progress.* New York: Doubleday, Doran, 1944.

Stone, Irving. *Clarence Darrow for the Defense.* New York: Doubleday, 1941.

Stuart, John. *The Education of John Reed.* New York: International Publications, 1955.

Symes, Lillian, and Travers Clement. *Rebel America: The Story of Social Revolt in the United States.* New York: Harper, 1934.

Taft, Philip. *The A.F. of L. in the Time of Gompers.* New York: Harper, 1957.

Thomas, Norman. *A Socialist's Faith.* New York: W. W. Norton, 1951.

Thompson, Fred. *The I.W.W.: Its First Fifty Years.* Chicago: International Workers of the World, 1955.

Trachtenberg, Alexander, ed. *The American Labor Year Book, 1919-1920.* New York: Rand School, 1920.

Van Der Slice, Austin. *International Labor, Diplomacy, and Peace.* Philadelphia: University of Pennsylvania Press, 1941.

Villard, Oswald G. *Fighting Years: Memoirs of a Fighting Editor.* New York: Harcourt, Brace, 1939.

Whipple, Leon. *The Story of Civil Liberty in the United States.* New York: Vanguard, 1927.

Wittke, Carl. *German Americans and the World War.* Columbus: Ohio State Archeological and Historical Society, 1936.

Wreszin, Michael. *Oswald Villard: Pacifist at War.* Bloomington: University of Indiana Press, 1965.

Zaretz, Charles E. *The Amalgamated Clothing Workers of America.* New York: Ancon Press, 1934.

Letters and Interview

Bassett, T. D. Seymour, Dec. 12, 1962, to author.
Eastman, Max, Oct. 31, 1960, to author.
Link, Arthur S., Sept. 29, 1964, to author.
Lochner, Louis P., Aug. 19, 1961, to author.
Nearing, Scott, Oct. 26, 1960, to author.
Panken, Jacob, Oct. 18, 1965, to author.
Thomas, Norman, June 2, 1961, to author.
————, interview, July 7, 1964, New York City.

Newspapers

Albany (N.Y.) *Telegram*, May 12, 1917.
Chicago *Daily News*, Sept. 8, 1917.
Miller's Weekly (New York), July 6, 1917.
New York *Analyst*, June 18, 1917.
New York *Call*, 1912-1920.
New York *Daily Tribune*, July 13, 1906.
New York *Jewish Morning Journal*, Sept. 7, 1917.
New York *Times*, 1914-1920.
Washington *Herald*, May 12, 1917.
Worcester *Times*, May 11, 1917.

Public Documents

American Federation of Labor: History, Encyclopedia, References. Washington, D.C.: American Federation of Labor Publication House, 1919.
American Federation of Labor, *Proceedings*, 37th annual convention, Buffalo, N.Y., Nov. 1917; 38th annual convention, St. Paul, Minn., June, 1918. Washington, D.C.: Law Reporter Printing Co.
Congressional Record, Senate, 65th Congress, first session, Aug., 1917.
————, Senate, 65th Congress, first session, Sept., 1917.
————, House of Representatives, 65th Congress, second session, Jan. 11, 1918.
————, House of Representatives, 65th Congress, second session, July, 1918.

Index